Mathilde Favier

Living Beautifully in Paris

Text
Frédérique Dedet

Photographs
Pascal Chevallier

Flammarion

FRONTISPIECE
Gilles Dufour with (from
left to right) Charlotte
Deffe, Camille Miceli,
Mathilde Favier, and
Pauline Favier on Place de
la Concorde. Photograph
by Grey Zisser, published
in the first issue of
CHANEL magazine, 1993.
PAGES 2–3
Portrait of Mathilde by
Vanessa Seward, 2021.
FACING PAGE
Paris ceramic vase by
Astier de Villatte.

Contents

Her good humor is legendary, her energy infectious, her loyalty unwavering, and everyone in her orbit falls under her spell. As PR manager for Dior Couture, in charge of celebrities worldwide, she always dedicates the same attention to everyone—artists, actresses, politicians, first ladies, queens, or pop stars—and has the knack of always knowing what will suit them best.

Mathilde is a Parisienne to the tips of her perfectly manicured fingernails. She loves people, loves to open up every door and possibility for them, to entertain them with her inimitable flair and mix them with others whom she has taken to her generous heart. When she discovers somewhere new she will take all her friends there. Her presence is irresistible, her elegance inspiring, her taste flawless, and her choices influential.

There's nothing she won't do for her loved ones, be they her children, lovers, family, or close friends. The life she enjoys with them—filled with beauty, joy, and fun—is also the product of unrelenting perfectionism. For behind all that fun and frivolity lies a discipline that commands respect, an uncompromisingly high standard that she demands only of herself.

Mathilde is one of those people who never forgets a birthday, who will invite a friend who is on her own to come for Christmas, who will move heaven and earth to get a friend an urgent appointment with an eminent medical specialist. Her friendship is precious and very special, her cheerfulness is contagious, and her advice is always sound.

The Paris that Mathilde has chosen to show us in these pages is in her image, beautiful, joyful, and chic. She shares what it is that, for her, really *makes* Paris, what really matters.

This book doesn't set out to bombard readers with advice or admonitions: it is a delightful stroll on which Mathilde introduces us to the people and places that make Paris the most beautiful city in the world.

And it is not a guidebook either, but an encapsulation of all that Mathilde loves about Paris.

Frédérique Dedet

FACING PAGE
Mathilde leaves the house in the Paris rain, wearing a smile and a Dior blouson jacket designed for JISOO and given to her by the singer.

Foreword

I thought of this book as a way of preserving a particular idea of Paris, and of an *art de vivre* that has been passed down to me. The familiar ways and customs of my Parisian childhood are still with me, shaping the way I am, and I wanted to gift them to future generations. The watchwords of my upbringing could be love, quality, refinement, and beauty, but also freedom. Freedom of speech mattered, and nothing was taboo.

At home, my mother would never leave the butter in its wrapper or price tags on anything, would always make sure we sent handwritten thank-you notes, and made my grandfather's motto her own: "I'm not rich enough to skimp." Everything she bought was good quality, and she instilled in us her great love of entertaining. We were surrounded by beautiful things.

When I was still very young, I was lucky enough to be introduced to a world that no longer exists. At sixteen, I made the paper tablecloths for the wedding of Édouard and Arielle de Rothschild at the Hôtel Lambert. Marie-Hélène de Rothschild invited me to the wedding ball as a thank you, and I went with my Uncle Gilles. Madeleine Castaing, who was incredibly charming, often came to tea with us; she adored my mother (and was fond of Pauline and me). Jacqueline de Ribes became a friend after we rented her houses. Lee Radziwill introduced me to my future husband, and we were married in Giovanni Volpi's palazzo on the Giudecca. And I would often have supper on Sundays with the Lalannes at Ury.

This notion of quality and beauty, so deeply rooted in my DNA, has only grown stronger from closer contact. It affects every aspect of my life, which is doubtless why I work in the luxury sector. I'm as exacting about things as I am about my friendships and relationships. I give a great deal and I receive a great deal.

The people we meet in these pages all represent different pieces of the jigsaw puzzle that makes up Paris. With their talents and their different worlds, they impart a unique flavor to *my* city. Like the people I grew up with, they come from all sorts of backgrounds, and they all have talent, imagination, taste, and refinement. All Parisians in their own unique way, they all add to the beauty of the city and of life.

Mathilde

FACING PAGE
Mathilde with her mother, Françoise Favier, and her daughter, Héloïse Agostinelli: three women, three generations of the art of smiling.

A Parisian
Childhood

B orn under the horse chestnut trees of the 16th arrondissement, Mathilde has always had a deep attachment to her neighborhood. Her mother and her uncle both live close by, and before her sisters moved to the Left Bank they, too, were her neighbors for many years. Her life is rooted in this leafy, sheltered triangle, where she knows every street, and where she enjoyed an equally protected childhood. Her school life passed uneventfully at the Institut de l'Assomption, known as the Lübeck after the street on which it stands, the girls' school (now coeducational) where her mother went before her—and which set the boys dreaming at the end of every school day. The navy-and-white uniform, accessorized with thick woolen tights in winter and lacy white ankle socks in the spring, was compulsory. There Mathilde made lifelong friendships with girls who—can it be a coincidence?—all grew up to become major figures in fashion: Camille Miceli, Vanessa Seward, and Emmanuelle Alt.

From her childhood, she remembers the family apartment on Rue Octave-Feuillet, a paean to Madeleine Castaing, the great antique dealer and interior designer whose style is still celebrated today. Amid the costumes for the musical comedies she and her cousins used to stage, she grew up in what was practically an all-female household, surrounded by her parents and her sisters: Victoire, her idol and fairy godmother—seven years older than her, and half-sister from her mother's first marriage to Antoine de Castellane—and Pauline, her younger sister, born eighteen months after her to the day.

The week was punctuated by dance lessons with Madame Barre (you couldn't make it up) at the Théâtre des Champs-Élysées, trips with her Uncle Gilles to the swimming pool on Boulevard Lannes, Wednesday lunch at her grandmother's house on Avenue d'Eylau, hot chocolate on the Place du Trocadéro, where Madame Carette reigned supreme at the cash register, fulminating to anyone who would listen about the times they lived in and the root problem: "There's no money any more, just cash!"

She was not yet fourteen when her uncle Gilles Dufour, her mother's younger brother and Karl Lagerfeld's right-hand man at the time, arranged her first internship at Chanel. There she met another teenager, Sofia Coppola, with whom she would always stay in touch, even appearing in her film *Marie Antoinette*. Naturally elegant, the young Mathilde was now launched like a debutante, and her cheerfulness was already legendary. With the charm and adventurousness she had inherited and the style and confidence she had absorbed from her upbringing, she could navigate her way through all weathers and every social situation. Nothing and nobody daunted her, and she was able to adapt and learn from everyone and everything.

After her baccalaureate in economics, she was obsessed with one thing: earning her own living. It wasn't long before she gave up her language studies at the Institut Catholique de Paris and the École du Louvre to take up an internship her Uncle Gilles had arranged for her with Brigitte Langevin and Anne Chabrol at *Glamour* magazine, Condé Nast's trendy "baby *Vogue.*" There, she met everyone who was anyone in the fashion world, photographers, top models, fashion editors, and journalists, including Mario Testino, Juergen Teller, David LaChapelle, Jean-Baptiste Mondino, Babeth Djian, and Carine Roitfeld.

Ready to turn her hand to anything, Mathilde now took on a series of different roles as part of this talented editorial team. As head of news, then assistant to the editor-in-chief and to the fashion editor, she picked up the founding principles that still hold true for her profession today: "The lessons I learned from Anne Chabrol are still with me."

Ever since her childhood, Mathilde has lived to the rhythms of Paris.

PAGE 10
The carousel next to the Eiffel Tower.
PAGE 11
Tucked into the frame of a mirror—a flea market find—in Françoise Favier's home, black-and-white photographs of her three daughters, Mathilde, Pauline, and Victoire.
FACING PAGE
A montage of family photographs: Mathilde with her sisters, from her happy Parisian childhood to schoolgirl and life as a young woman.

LA REINE MATHILDE

En haut, elle est morte de rire en combinaison dorée **Magic Circle** ; pêle-mêle : photos "de famille" ; à g., fausse fourrure imitation singe, le tout **Chanel**.

Mathilde n'est pas le style de fille à faire tapisserie le soir, ni le jour d'ailleurs. Vêtue de la tête aux pieds presque exclusivement **Chanel** – son oncle et sa sœur sont des sommités du studio de couture –, elle se moque pas mal de faire sensation dans les salons et préfère de loin – et de près aussi – se faire siffler dans les rues de Paris. Frange des faubourgs, taille de guêpe (son animal fétiche ; elle s'est fait

De hau[...] son lit [...] Chanel [...] redingo[...] Apostro[...] Marzia [...] dans se[...] porte u[...] Sitbon [...]

PAGES 14–15, LEFT TO RIGHT
Page from the "1 fille, 1 style" feature in *Glamour* magazine, July 1995, under the headline *La Reine Mathilde*; polaroid of Mathilde with her sister Pauline; Gilles Dufour with (back row, left to right) Marie-Camille Duval, Mathilde Favier, Camille Miceli, and Fanfan Bouscasse, and (front row, left to right) Belem Canovas, Charlotte Deffe, and Pauline Favier in Coco Chanel's apartment, photograph by Grey Zisser for the first issue of *CHANEL* magazine, 1993; portrait of Mathilde painted by Marc-Antoine Coulon; photograph of Mathilde by Manuela Pavesi, styled by Anna Dello Russo for Italian *Glamour* magazine.
LEFT
Cigarette break 1772-style, during the filming of *Marie Antoinette* by Sofia Coppola: Mathilde with Fifi Chachnil and Al Weaver. Photograph by Andrew Durham, 2005.
PAGES 18–19
A girl, a style: a selection of Mathilde's daily selfies in the elevator on the way up to her office.

"When I was still very young, I was lucky enough to be introduced to a world that no longer exists." – Mathilde

BELOW
Mathilde wearing a Christian Dior trench coat with the iconic *Plan de Paris* motif, laid out around Avenue Montaigne and inspired by the Dior archives.

FACING PAGE
Mathilde, radiant in a silk satin shirt from the Inde de Christian Dior collection, Lady Dior collector bag, and Furlanes Mary Janes Black Satin Venetian slippers from Chatelles Paris.

Gilles Dufour
(her uncle)

Gilles Dufour is a stylist and artistic director. After graduating from the École des Arts Décoratifs in Paris, he worked in top Paris fashion houses including Chanel, Fendi, and Balmain. He has launched his own label and designed costumes and sets for the theater, cinema, and opera: for the Fenice in Venice, Rudolf Nureyev at the Opéra Garnier, and the cast of the musical comedy *Mayflower*.

He was present at the grand balls thrown by Café Society throughout the world. He currently exercises his talents with Erdos, a major Chinese fashion label with two thousand boutiques in Asia.

His apartment, with furniture upholstered by Decour (upholsterer and interior designer to Nissim de Camondo), is piled high with books, hung with paintings by Neo-Romantic artists, and perfumed with Cuir by Diptyque or Maharajah by Nicolaï, mingled with the scents of the flowers he adores.

Very close to his nieces, he taught Mathilde how to navigate the world.

"He has an ultra-chic attitude and excellent taste, and he has a great sense of humor and is very cultured," confides Mathilde. "Gilles is curious about everything. These were the foundations on which I built my career and my life, in fact. He's unique."

FAR LEFT
Gilles Dufour in his living room, engulfed by books, paintings, objets, and family photographs.
LEFT
La Pensée, an original plaster bust by Henri Chapu, presides over the marble mantelpiece.

For Gilles, Paris is:
"Dining in a good restaurant, visiting the Louvre
and the Orangerie, hunting for treasures at the
Marché aux Puces, going to the theater and the opera,
marking the passing seasons with flowers from
his favorite florists."

LEFT
A clutch of stuffed
animals on an armchair
covered in tiger-skin
velvet by Le Manach.
ABOVE
Photograph of Gilles
by Pierre et Gilles, 1979.
FACING PAGE
Plaster cast from
a school in Nancy.

ABOVE
Gilles's world: a
Pre-Raphaelite tondo,
lampshades by his friend
Pierre Le-Tan, birds from
Deyrolle, and flowers,
for which he often travels
as far as Thalie in the
5th arrondissement or the
flower market in Rungis.

RIGHT
The breakfast table set
with an English service
from Au Bain Marie,
a Herren jug, Joy by Rohan
Chabot glasses, and a
vintage Porthault cloth.

FACING PAGE
Portrait of Gilles by Karl
Lagerfeld, propped on a
velvet-covered armchair.

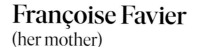

Françoise Favier
(her mother)

With her youthful figure and dancer's posture,
Mathilde's mother is the embodiment of charm,
of lightness, both literally and figuratively. The soul of
kindness, she always sees the good in everyone and
always has a friendly word. "It's that carefree spirit that
shields her from everything," says her daughter.
Born in Lyon, Françoise came to Paris when her father
got a job as a stockbroker in the year of the New Look—
little suspecting that two of her daughters would work for
Dior! The family made their home on Avenue d'Eylau,
where she lived until she got married.

An antique dealer manqué who has filled her apartment with treasures unearthed early on Fridays at the Marché aux Puces, she has trained her three daughters to have an eye for beauty, just as she passed on her perfect upbringing, elegance, and kindness. Madeleine Castaing adored her, and Lee Radziwill became her close friend when she moved to Paris. Working well beyond retirement age, Françoise devotes her unique expertise to welcoming and advising clients at Au Bain Marie, her gorgeous boutique brimming with original ideas for stylish entertaining, gentle and child-like, just like her.

"I'm accustomed to the beauty of Paris and I couldn't live without it, even if sadly it's no longer the Paris of my childhood."

"I love the Jardin des Plantes, the bouquinistes, and the glasshouses of Paris."

FACING PAGE
Françoise's bedroom. The fabrics on the bed are from her daughter Pauline's label, Bloom Paris.

LEFT AND ABOVE
Françoise's apartment on Rue Octave-Feuillet in Paris, where Mathilde grew up, as seen in a feature by Pascal Hinous in *Maison & Jardin* in May 1985, and a photograph of Françoise. "She lives in a childhood world," says Mathilde, "a world of rabbits and barbotine figurines, the enchanted world of Beatrix Potter."

Victoire de Castellane
(her half-sister)

Twenty-five years ago, with her huge talent, unique style, and brimming imagination, Victoire invented Dior Joaillerie. As a child, Mathilde's older half-sister was fascinated by the jewelry worn by the women around her, her Hennessy grandmother and her friend Barbara Hutton, as well as the jewels she dreamed of. At twelve, she had her first communion and christening medals melted down to make her first ring. At twenty-one, she gave up her nights at Le Palace nightclub, where her style did not go unnoticed, to join Chanel. There she designed costume jewelry, alongside Karl Lagerfeld and her uncle Gilles Dufour, and also did some modeling. But when Bernard Arnault offered her carte blanche to create Dior Joaillerie she couldn't resist. With her colored stones, opals, themes, volumes, improbable mixes, and the sheer flamboyance of her creations, Victoire made jewelry history. The liberty, daring, sincerity, and humor of it all turned the muted codes of Place Vendôme on their heads—and remains true for each new collection, which always has a wonderful story to tell.

Victoire: "Paris is a city of pastel tones, with all those marvelous grays, from the pinkest to the darkest. What lends Paris color is the light, like the light on the stone in a jewel."

Mathilde: "What I admire most about Victoire is her modesty. She's still shy despite her huge talent. She brought about a revolution by giving women the freedom to wear statement jewelry in the daytime without ever looking ridiculous, and to buy it for themselves."

LEFT AND ABOVE
Self-portrait and collage
by Victoire.
TOP
The Ancolia Veneinosa
Pop ring, in yellow gold,
diamonds, fire opal, yellow,
orange, and pink sapphires,
spinels, Ethiopian white
opal, tsavorite garnets, and
lacquer, from the Belladone
Island collection created
by Victoire for Dior
Joaillerie.

FACING PAGE
A tree of life created
as a gift for Françoise,
and a photograph
of Victoire by
François Halard.

34.

Maman que j'aime

Victoire

Pauline Favier-Henin
(her sister)

They are as different in character as they are in appearance. Pauline began her career in television, with Canal+ and later Paris Première. During an extended stopover in Pondicherry, in the middle of a world tour with her husband and their two children, she fell in love with Indian fabrics and an idea for starting her own business began to take shape. In 2017, she gave up her television career and founded Bloom Paris. Her stylish bed and table linens, tableware, and clothing for adults and, more recently, children have taken off, with an online shop, a Paris boutique, and US pop-ups in Aerin Lauder stores from the Hamptons to Palm Beach. "We're very different, but we can't do without each other," says Mathilde, summing up a relationship founded on the unbreakable bond of their shared childhood and their deep sisterly affection.

"For me, the 7th arrondissement is a little piece of the countryside in Paris, since where I live is surrounded by trees and greenery. Forget the car. Walking around here is great. The Rodin Museum is one of my favorite museums. And in my view Bon Marché with its Grande Épicerie is the most beautiful of all French *grands magasins*. The gorgeous boulangerie at 112 Rue Saint-Dominique makes the best bread in the neighborhood."

FACING PAGE
Pauline in her apartment in the 7th arrondissement, in front of a table by Bruno Capacci.
INSET
A sample of one of the fabulous fabrics made in India that inspired her Bloom Paris collections.
LEFT AND ABOVE
Pauline's Indo-Parisian world, chic and cosmopolitan.

Paris, *City of Fashion*

P aris is the most beautiful city in the world. Its architecture, its harmony, its light—everything here inspires creativity and beauty, whether in painting, literature, or, naturally, fashion. And the first to fall under the spell of its beauty are the Parisians themselves.

According to Jean-Baptiste Colbert, minister and trusted advisor to Louis XIV, "Fashion is to France what the gold mines of Peru are to Spain." Which is still true over three centuries later: Paris is the undisputed world capital of fashion. It was the birthplace of the first couture house, founded in 1858 by Charles Frederick Worth, an Englishman who chose the city for his firm. After him, designers the world over dreamed of setting up their businesses in the City of Light.

On January 23, 1945, haute couture became an *appellation* protected by law, and today, only sixteen houses can boast of meeting the criteria required for membership of this ultra-exclusive circle, which includes the likes of Dior, Chanel, and Valentino. Their collections, made by hand in their own ateliers, are shown in Paris Haute Couture Week, in January and July every year.

The ready-to-wear fashion shows take place during Paris Fashion Week, held four times a year, in January and June for menswear, and in late February and late September for womenswear.

During Fashion Week, Paris is buzzing. The whole world, including celebrities from around the globe, flocks to the French capital. The city's restaurants and hotels are packed, and every day is a round of fashion shows, presentations, cocktail parties, and dinners. It's intense, but it's fun! For Mathilde, "I dedicate this time to Dior. It is nonstop: I greet guests, I dress them, I take care of them, and I do it twenty-four hours a day, as though I'm throwing a dinner party at home that goes on for a whole week! Paris is buzzing with excitement, it's sheer joy."

PAGE 38
A Stockman mannequin in the Dior couture ateliers.
PAGE 39
A look from the Christian Dior Spring–Summer 2024 haute couture show.
ABOVE
The Tableau Final gala ball gown in white tulle, embellished with garlands of hollyhocks, Naturelle line, Spring–Summer 1951 haute couture collection. Photograph by Willy Maywald.
FACING PAGE
Mathilde in Dior pajamas on the stairs leading up from the showroom to her office, during the weeks of intense activity leading up to Fashion Week.

Mathilde and photographers
at the Musée Rodin
during the Dior Spring–
Summer 2023 haute
couture show.

"Every day of my life, Maria Grazia inspires me with her ideas, her designs, her values, her sense of humor, her intelligence, her taste." – Mathilde

LEFT
A look from the Autumn–Winter 2023 haute couture collection by Maria Grazia Chiuri, Creative Director of womenswear and accessories at the House of Dior since 2016.

BELOW
Backstage, makeup is always by Peter Philips, Belgian Creative Director of Dior Makeup since 2014.

FACING PAGE
Mathilde with Maria Grazia Chiuri in January 2023.

LEFT
Photographers on the lookout for celebrity guests at the Dior Spring–Summer 2023 haute couture show.

PAGES 48–49
The fabulous décor
for the Dior Autumn–
Winter 2023–2024
ready-to-wear show,
designed by the Portuguese
artist Joana Vasconcelos.
The ready-to-wear
collections are presented
in a "Dior nightclub"
in the Tuileries Gardens,
while the haute couture
collections are shown in
the gardens of the Musée
Rodin. Every season,
a new décor is conceived
by artists around the
theme of the collection.

ABOVE
A model photographed
backstage, and the famous
Japanese twin sisters of
J-Pop, Ami and Aya Suzuki
of the Amiaya duo, who
never miss a Dior show.
RIGHT
A look from the Dior
Spring–Summer 2024
haute couture show.

La Galerie Dior

Since March 2022, 30 Avenue Montaigne has been home to this unique exhibition space, bearing witness to the visionary daring of Christian Dior and his six successors: Yves Saint Laurent, Marc Bohan, Gianfranco Ferré, John Galliano, Raf Simons, and Maria Grazia Chiuri. The designs, photographs, and objets assembled with passion in this magical place enable visitors to immerse themselves in the fabulous history of the House of Dior.

LEFT
The spectacular spiral staircase leading up to the exhibition spaces in La Galerie Dior, symbol of Paris haute couture. Winding up through a rainbow display of 452 dresses and 1,422 accessories, it plunges the visitor into an extraordinary colorama of dresses, bags, and shoes. The spirit of Christian Dior is tangible still. "He is here, because he walked through all these spaces," says Nathalie Crinière, the interior designer and scenographer who designed La Galerie Dior.

PAGES 54–55
Héloïse Agostinelli, Mathilde's daughter, photographed at the Dior exhibition at The Musée des Arts Décoratifs by Tom Watson for Spanish *Glamour* in October 2017.

At *Home*

E ntertaining at home is a characteristically Parisian pastime, with the idea of home becoming ever more important in the city. Paris apartments, many of them dating back several hundred years, have seen structural alterations prompted by major social changes and the blending of worlds that were once separate: men and women, parents and children, employers and domestic staff. Adapted by talented architects, they have been redesigned to suit new lifestyles.

But whether Parisians live in fifteenth-century houses (a few of which still survive), seventeenth-century mansions, or apartment blocks built by the ruthless genius of Baron Haussmann or dating from the 1930s, they all like to welcome guests into their homes. In Paris, hosts happily welcome guests even into the privacy of the kitchen, now the hub of city apartments. There, the art of conversation, so dear to the French, can flourish, whether in debates or confidential discussions: nothing is off limits.

Whereas until the 1960s couples would marry and furnish their homes to last a lifetime, nowadays the trend is to redecorate to keep up with fashions or new passions. And Paris is the ideal place for it, being home to a concentration of the finest experts in the French decorative arts: the world's leading artisans in wood, stone, marble, metal, wool, and gilding; the world's finest silversmiths and ceramists specializing in tableware; and the world's leading fabric designers. And all this exceptional savoir-faire is complemented by the skills of the world's most talented interior designers.

The interiors shown here, from Mathilde's own home to those of prominent figures in their various domains, are all iconic examples of Parisian homes.

ABOVE
On the mantelpiece, Victoire's first picture, a gift to her sister Mathilde.

FACING PAGE
Mathilde's kitchen, with its window opening on to the courtyard, is another living space, like so many other kitchens in Paris.

PAGE 56
A picture of the Arc de Triomphe—a flea market find—in Mathilde's hallway.

PAGE 57
Mathilde on her balcony in a Dior evening dress. "Azzedine Alaïa used to say that after forty you shouldn't show your legs or your arms, but Maria Grazia's dresses allow you to rise to the challenge."

PAGES 60–61
Mathilde's dining room is a homage to Lee Radziwill's London drawing room, designed by Renzo Mongiardino in the 1960s. The table is set with plates by Maria Grazia Chiuri for Dior Maison.

PAGES 62–63
A compilation of sublime table settings. Whether for a formal dinner or simple breakfast, Mathilde always dresses her tables with love. Lots of candles shed a warm, flattering glow, and fresh flowers decorate the table and escape into the whole apartment. An expert in the art of mix and match, Mathilde cleverly mingles heirloom china and glasses and flea market finds with more contemporary designs— although coordinating the tablecloth with her outfit is emphatically not her style!

FACING PAGE, TOP
A collection of candlesticks by Pauline Vincent, founder of the online boutique La Romaine Éditions, selling quirky and original designs for the home.

FACING PAGE, LEFT
Mathilde with chef Philippe Ragot, a family friend for many years.

FACING PAGE, BELOW
Mathilde likes to introduce up-and-coming chefs to her guests. On this occasion, she has asked Angèle Ferreux-Maeght to cater for a dinner. The great-granddaughter of Aimé and Marguerite Maeght on her mother's side and great-niece of Jean-Louis Trintignant on her father's, Angèle has created La Guinguette d'Angèle, offering indulgent gluten-free dishes that have proved a huge success. With two locations in Paris, she also offers an online grocery store, plus a catering service for every occasion.

"I adore the vegan dishes from La Guinguette d'Angèle. I enjoy giving opportunities to young chefs and I love introducing my guests to their cooking."

BELOW
Pauline Vincent engulfed by armfuls of mimosa supplied by Éric Chauvin.

"My house is like an old English lady, it had to have chintz!
I was very inspired by Hauteville House, the house on
Guernsey where Victor Hugo lived in exile, where every room
has a different atmosphere and tells a different story." – Mathilde

FACING PAGE
A photograph by Mario
Testino, brought back from
Lima by Mathilde's partner,
and a collection of Clichy
glass vases found in flea
markets by her mother,
Françoise.

"And yet I'm not one to *vider mon sac*." — **Mathilde**

LEFT
Mathilde has turned the laundry room into an office, where she can think and keep all her secrets.
FACING PAGE
The Dior crochet tote bag that holds all Mathilde's essential accessories.

Jacques Grange
and Pierre Passebon

Their apartment in the Palais Royal, once home to
Colette, is the perfect expression of Jacques Grange's
taste, a French style of which Paris is the custodian.
Fresh from the École Boulle and the École
Camondo, he became assistant to Henri Samuel,
the design legend who decorated chateau interiors
for patrons including William Randolph Hearst,
the Rothschilds, and Valentino.

Taken under the wing of Marie-Laure de Noailles, the man who
is among the world's most famous interior designers adopted the
mantra of another of his patrons, Madeleine Castaing: "In decoration
you should always evoke, never reconstruct."

He applied this principle with great skill in all the residences of
Yves Saint Laurent and Pierre Bergé, while other loyal and enthusiastic
clients include Terry and Jean de Gunzburg, Israel Englander, and
a number of hotels, including the legendary Mark Hotel in New York
and Francis Ford Coppola's Palazzo Margherita in Italy.

His interiors reflect the harmonious relationships he enjoys with
his clients, almost all of whom are friends. A born storyteller with an
infallible memory, Jacques always has a fund of fascinating tales to tell.

Mathilde has known this childhood friend of her uncle Gilles
Dufour all her life. When her American former husband told her
that Jacques was going to decorate their apartment, she remembers,
"I was impressed and astonished—not many people in Paris go
to an interior designer. Jacques won me over straight away. He taught
me to buy intelligently, not to fall into the trap of clichés, and not
to be afraid of buying expensive things either!"

"You don't explain Jacques's interior designs, you feel them." — Pierre Passebon

ABOVE
The "Jacques a dit" years.
Mathilde and Jacques
Grange, photographed
by François Halard
on the shocking pink
Chesterfield in Mathilde's
apartment.
FACING PAGE
Mathilde in 2006, in her
apartment decorated
by Jacques.

La Galerie du Passage

It was as long ago as 1991 that Pierre Passebon moved into the Galerie Véro-Dodat, without doubt the most remarkable shopping arcade in Paris, close to the Palais Royal. Christian Louboutin then followed suit, opening his first boutique at the Rue Jean-Jacques-Rousseau end. With his bold, confident taste, Pierre offers furniture and objets from the twentieth century to the present day. He was the first to show Jean Royère, Alexandre Noll, and Gio Ponti. He has a particular passion for ceramics, and exhibits the work of Giuseppe Ducrot, Bela Silva, and Clémentine de Chabaneix. Karl Lagerfeld, David Lynch, Lynn Davis, and Bruce Weber have all chosen him to show their photographs. He is also a staunchly loyal friend. His collection of original comic strip plates has been exhibited at the New National Museum of Monaco, and he owns the largest collection of portraits of Marlène Dietrich—a true obsession—which has been shown at the Maison Européenne de la Photographie in Paris and now at the International Center of Photography in New York. Collectors from all over the world can be sure always to find something original at the Galerie du Passage.

"He has a very sure eye and a wicked sense of humor, and he is unshockable," says Mathilde. "A subtle psychologist, he has preserved an aspect of childhood that I find very touching."

PAGES 76–77, FACING PAGE, AND ABOVE
Galerie Passebon, in the magnificent Véro-Dodat shopping arcade in the 1st arrondissement.
LEFT
Victoire de Castellane, Mathilde's older sister, with her husband, Thomas Lenthal, at a private view in the Galerie du Passage.

Terry de Gunzburg

She has given makeup its pedigree, first with Yves Saint Laurent and then with her own label, By Terry, and she spreads beauty all around her. Her Paris home—the first commission carried out by the young Hector Guimard—displays her powerful love of color and texture, in a dazzling ensemble created with her friend Jacques Grange in which different periods are combined and every painting, piece of furniture, and objet is of museum quality. An informed, loyal, and generous collector, Terry entertains in eastern style—she was born in Egypt—and creates wonderful table settings. "You only ever see plates and glasses like that at her house. Her delicious dinners are always very entertaining, with a clever mix of interesting characters. I admire the career path of this woman, a mother of four children, who has always worked. I respect her taste, her innate sense of color, and her generous heart." If Paris were a color? "Flaming rose-red."

PAGES 80–81
A unique tapestry by Mattia Bonetti spread as a rug. "It's a touch of blush that lends a glow to the whole room, bright without being garish," says Terry.

BELOW
In the dining room, the table is set with plates that are a flea market find by Françoise Favier, Mathilde's mother.

The door surrounds by Alexandre Bigot, the ceramicist who worked for Hector Guimard, are from Jacques Grange's private collection. The glass doors were designed by Jacques and made by Les Ateliers de France.

FACING PAGE
Beside each other in the master bedroom, two masterpieces : a Biedermeier secretaire and an armchair by Paul Iribe.

Vincent Darré

Eternally young and a multitalented creative, Vincent has been brightening Paris life with his cheerfulness and good humor since his teenage years. Often described as a dandy—which he refutes—this epitome of elegance is a hive of industry with a thousand strings to his bow. Starting out as a stylist, after many years as Karl Lagerfeld's right-hand man at Fendi, he went on to work with some of the greatest Italian fashion houses. After the millennium, when he was artistic director at Ungaro, he left the fashion world and moved into interior design and decoration. In no time, the success of Maison Darré, on Rue du Mont-Thabor, and its surrealist designs, led to a commission for the interiors of the Schiaparelli couture salons on Place Vendôme and a string of other projects.

His expertise in the decorative arts needs no introduction. After living on Rue de Bellechasse for many years he was keen to move, but wanted to stay in the area. By a stroke of luck, he found this quirky, dual-aspect apartment at the end of the Cité de Varenne enclave, which he was able to redecorate throughout during lockdown, so creating the ideal setting for many more dreams to come true.

84.

FACING PAGE
Vincent places a candle
in the sumptuous 1940s
Murano glass chandelier in
his kitchen–dining room,
with its trompe-l'oeil
painted tent decoration.
The table set for his guests
stands on a rug from
Casa Lopez, while the
Italian chairs were a flea
market find. "He's always
enthusiastic, always full
of fun, with a playful side
that's hugely attractive.
What I love about him
is the Parisian Charlie
Chaplin in him,"
says Mathilde.

ABOVE
The nineteenth-century
Italian bed in the master
bedroom, upholstered and
covered in a fabric from
Hutton Wilkinson, is
perfectly complemented
by the wallpaper designed
by Vincent himself
and produced by
Au Fil des Couleurs.

RIGHT
A collection of objets
arranged on an Italian
baroque gueridon.

PAGES 86–87
In the living-room
fireplace, beside a coffee
table from his own
Renaissance collection,
a nineteenth-century
settee covered in a Pierre
Frey fabric sits against the
wall facing the fireplace,
on which stands a pair
of eighteenth-century
wooden busts.
"Vincent has a gift for
mixing his own designs
with family furniture
and souvenirs from close
friends" says Mathilde.

Brenda Altmayer

"Coming to Paris for love, she stayed for the love of Paris."
Direct and charming, this Spanish Basque interior
designer lives with her husband, the film producer
Éric Altmayer, in the heart of Saint-Germain-des-Prés.
The apartment was formerly designed by Pierre
Passebon for Florence Grinda, and Brenda has cleverly
kept the doors and moldings, and, above all, the amazing
fireplace made from a collection of Italian tiles. When
she redecorated Mathilde's apartment a few years ago,
she made Mathilde's dream come true by creating a
dining room inspired by the one Renzo Mongiardino
designed for Lee Radziwill in London in the 1960s.

Mathilde: "Life has gifted her to me like a sister-in-law.
I think she's beautiful to begin with, and incredibly
inspiring. We redecorated my apartment together and
had a lot of fun." Brenda adds: "After decades in Paris,
after having two sons in Paris, I still feel a bit of an outsider,
and I still observing Parisians with a detached eye."

LEFT
In the entrance hall,
an object now typical
of Parisian apartments:
a bicycle!
ABOVE
The old neo-Gothic
doors have been preserved
in the living room.
FACING PAGE
Brenda on her sublime
fire surround.

88.

Aurélie Bidermann

She has lived several lives. A jewelry designer with her own label for over ten years, she has had boutiques in Paris and New York, where she lived for a time. Her original designs—braided necklaces, cocktail rings, mother-of-pearl elephants—were snapped up by an enthusiastic clientele. Nowadays, Aurélie Bidermann is an artistic director who is very much in demand. In September 2023, she created a wonderful collection called Babylone for Christofle. Since 1830, this Parisian firm has created outstanding tableware in collaboration with the finest master goldsmiths of the age and their ancestral savoir-faire. Aurélie lives in Paris, where her eight-year-old daughter, Rose, was born. "Paris has always been a source of inspiration for me, my muse in a way."

ABOVE
Designer Aurélie Bidermann in the Christofle boutique, Rue Royale.
RIGHT AND FACING PAGE
With the generous curves and clean lines of its braiding recalling plump brioche loaves, this collection of ultra-desirable pieces, from tableware to decorative objets and jewelry, is a master stroke of design. Created by Aurélie Bidermann for Christofle, the range has proved a runaway success.

Linda Pinto

She's the friend everyone should have. Strong, generous, caring, and organized, Linda is also the embodiment of elegance and beauty. Sister of the great interior designer Alberto Pinto, she worked at his side, and after his death in 2012 presided over his firm for a decade. In that role, she ensured that the lavish decorative schemes designed by Alberto's loyal collaborators and crafted by the finest Parisian artisans were seen throughout the world.

No one entertains like she does, devoting the same attention to detail however many guests she has invited, whether two or forty. She does everything herself, the flowers and table settings, and her cooking is divine—her couscous is the best.

"We have a number of mutual friends, including the distinguished oncologist Professor Alain Toledano. He treated me and he became my good friend. In 2018, he set up the Institut Rafaël in Paris, Europe's first center for integrative medicine. He also founded the Esthétique & Cancer association, with a mission to employ aesthetics and beauty to enable patients to maintain a strong link with the world 'outside' their illness. It's an initiative that I'm very proud to support."

LEFT
The chauffeuses in Linda's living room are covered in multicolored embroidery by the celebrated embroiderer Pascale Duchénoy.
BELOW
An excellent cook, Linda does all her own cooking for friends.
FACING PAGE
Linda in her kitchen with Mathilde and Dr Alain Toledano.

RIGHT
Linda's bathroom
originally belonged to
Loris Azzaro. Her brother
Alberto had it dismantled
and installed in his
Quai d'Orsay apartment,
where she lived for a long
time. Thanks to the
mirror-maker M. Gottardo,
she was able to move
it once again when
she moved into her new
apartment on the other
side of Les Invalides.

Elisabetta Beccari

Elisabetta is married to Pietro Beccari—CEO of Louis Vuitton—who was her teenage sweetheart when they were growing up together in Parma. After arriving in Paris seventeen years ago, she has raised their three daughters in the city and has collected around her a happy community of Italian women who have become Parisiennes for a variety of reasons. Her cooking is divine, and she is a magnificent and wonderfully generous hostess. Her sixteenth-century house is designed for entertaining.

PAGE 96
Two magnificent
Venini chandeliers in
Murano blown glass greet
visitors in Elisabetta
Beccari's hallway.

PAGE 97
Elisabetta with her 1920s
Berkel, which belonged to
her great-grandfather.

FACING PAGE AND ABOVE
The plant-filled courtyard
in the heart of Paris is
a meeting place for Italian
girlfriends who either live
in the city or are visiting.
With Elisabetta and
Mathilde are Isabella
Capece, Cristina Malgara,
Osanna Visconti,
and Gabriella Cortese.

Olivier Bialobos

So discreet that he doesn't want to be photographed,
so good a friend that he agrees to let his French bulldog,
Melchior, pose in his garden, Olivier is Deputy Managing
Director in charge of global communication and image
at Dior, where he arrived eighteen years ago, after rising
through the ranks at Escada and a brilliant career
with Tom Ford at Saint Laurent. With his expertise, he has
made a major contribution to the Dior image, gathering
together elements of the memory of Dior and bringing
it to life, while also bringing it into the present with
contemporary talents. He has developed Dior Héritage,
the archive collection that has made major exhibitions
around the world possible—from the Musée des Arts
Décoratifs in Paris to the V&A in London—and opened
La Galerie Dior in Paris, as well as staging memorable
fashion shows around the world. He is skilled at
reassuring artistic directors—of whom he has seen
a few—and at communicating with the press and with
his fellow directors. Funny, discerning, and cultured,
he has a big heart and is unfailingly loyal.

Mathilde: "Olivier is a friend. When I arrived at Dior
twelve years ago, he became my boss. With him, I learn
something new every day. He's hugely professional, a
driving force, and he has a vision. Fair and loyal with his
teams, he also really makes me laugh."

Olivier: "I often suggest to visitors that they should
go for a boat trip on the Seine to see Paris, it's magical.
And I take them to Montmartre, where I lived for a long
time: a true village in the heart of the capital, with all
its hidden treasures along Avenue Junot."

FACING PAGE
Handsome old stonework
surrounds Pierre Sauvage
on the magnificent
landing of his townhouse.
LEFT
A piece by Kim Moltzer,
with the Hôtel d'Orrouer
in the background.
BELOW
The Java print by Casa
Lopez, featuring two
birds hiding and playing
in dense foliage.
PAGE 104
The oak-paneled library,
with one of his three
shih tzus comfortably
installed on cushions
on a Casa Lopez carpet.
Who wouldn't dream
of being one of Pierre
Sauvage's dogs?
PAGE 105
On the mantelpiece
in the salon, a majestic
plaster bust of Henri II
stands under a chandelier
by Hervé Van der
Straeten, reflected to
infinity in the mirror.

Pierre Sauvage

After working as a press attaché for many years, Pierre embarked on a new life
when he took over Casa Lopez—chic, accessible, and ultra-Parisian despite its
name—and injected it with his own personality. Within a decade, this epicurean
aesthete transformed the carpet firm that first introduced rattan into middle-class
interiors into a lifestyle brand with the focus firmly on the art of entertaining.
Crazy about fabrics, he is also artistic director of Tissus Choisis par Casa Lopez,
with exclusivity on his favorite designers.

   His Paris apartment, reached up an imposing stone staircase, manages
to be simultaneously magnificent and intimate. Lying on the piano nobile of an
eighteenth-century townhouse on the Faubourg Saint-Germain, it offers a series
of dual-aspect salons, their walls lined with period wood paneling, with views
over one of the most beautiful private mansions in Paris, where Hubert
de Givenchy lived until the end of his life. Here, the spirit of classicism is given
a new twist by the color palette of the carpets and paintings, and above all by
the warmth of a home where the host welcomes guests with such great generosity.

   "For me, Paris is the Parc Montsouris of my childhood. And, more generally,
all the parks laid out in the nineteenth century, the Buttes-Chaumont and
the Bois de Boulogne. They are unique, evoking the Second Empire and Baron
Haussmann's transformation of the city into what Paris is still today."

Astier de Villatte

Standing apart from many older houses, Astier de Villatte was founded in 1996 by Ivan Pericoli and Benoît Astier de Villatte, young graduates of Paris's École des Arts Décoratifs who wanted to create *objets rêvés*. And so they dreamed up an array of furniture, tableware, and objets for the home in ceramic, to be joined a few years later by a range of perfumes and fragranced products.

Their reputation has spread by glowing word-of-mouth recommendations, and tables the world over are now graced by their white-glazed ceramic wares. Continuing to diversify, they have formed partnerships with artists (their large cat teapot by Setsuko is a marvel), worked with the ancestral workshops of Awaji Island in Japan, makers of the world's finest incense, launched a publishing house after acquiring a printing works, and recreated the world's oldest perfume, discovered on a papyrus. "A house that is distinctively Parisian in its creative freedom," far removed from any marketing diktats.

FACING PAGE
Astier de Villatte boutiques display magnificent objets in ceramic, made by hand in Paris.
RIGHT
Mathilde in the boutique on Rue de Tournon, where the ambience is unique, as in all their boutiques.

Laura Gonzalez

A talented interior designer who set up her own business straight after graduating, she has rapidly become a doyenne of mix and match, Paris-style. Laura creates asssemblages. She has recently moved into a house in the 16th arrondissement. Her flair for bohemian sophistication has captivated Cartier—for whom she has designed numerous boutiques around the world—and Christian Louboutin, as well as other legendary Parisian venues such as Lapérouse and the Saint James Hotel. An aficionado of the finest savoir-faire, she works with the most skilled of specialist artisans. Her colorful furniture is seen in the most select salons, and as proof of her iconic status in the new Parisian style, she has designed the Printemps store in New York. Here she invites us into her home/office, each floor with its own décor and theme.

Mathilde: "She has an irresistible energy, fun and addictive. Laura's style is something new in Paris. I just love it."

FACING PAGE
Laura's mix-and-match world, with a collection of Moroccan vases, and a stucco bas-relief of wisteria by Tollis.
RIGHT
Laura in her courtyard, beside her Madras armchair and a fountain created by Audrey Guimard, in association with Camille Coléon.

FACING PAGE
The Rainbow meeting
table, with its raku top
by specialist ceramicist
Fabienne L'Hostis,
surrounded by Mawu
chairs, with the Lilypad
chandelier in Murano glass.

The walls and ceiling
are painted with a décor
designed by Laura carried
out by Atelier Roma.
BELOW
A kinetic work designed
by Laura and made by
Bernard Pictet.

Three things she loves about Paris:
"Crossing the Pont des Arts at nightfall.
The Hôtel Raphaël, the only hotel not yet ruined by bad taste.
Strolling around the Nouvelle Athènes district in
the heart of the 9th arrondissement to admire the beauty
of the architecture."

RIGHT AND BELOW
Carolina's house is filled
with eclectic objects
from abroad, including
Suzani fabric from
Uzbekistan, red ceramic
from Mexico, and a green
Moroccan bowl filled
with coral branches in
Venetian glass.

FACING PAGE
An Indian dhurrie on
the floor, a sofa covered
with her Ciara fabric,
Turkish embroidered
cushions, and Iznik
plates on the wall above
large panels of
nineteenth-century
botanical drawings.

Carolina Irving

"She's a nomad in Paris, and her home is a reflection of herself,"
says Mathilde. Venezuelan but born in the United States and raised
in Paris, Carolina Irving designs for her own label of fabrics and
tableware with her two daughters. Based in New York for many years,
she worked as a stylist for *House & Garden* and *T Magazine*, among
others, and directed lines for Oscar de la Renta. Returning to Europe,
she played an active part in setting up Vermelho, her friend Christian
Louboutin's first hotel, in Melides, Portugal, where she owns
a stunning house. Her homes have featured in interior design
magazines the world over, and her taste is universally celebrated.
The living room of her Paris apartment—which she shares with her
husband, Bertrand Deveaud—showcases bohemian chic at its finest.
Cushions and lampshades in glorious fabrics, rugs, ceramics,
and furniture from all over the world, cleverly mixed with her own
designs, are all borrowed from different cultures and folk traditions.

Sophie Douzal

A serial entrepreneur, this mother of three with a wicked sense of humor runs the luxury PR and influencer agency she founded over twenty years ago. Two years ago, she also launched Le Château de Ma Mère, a brand that distils the Provençal *art de vivre* in the heart of Paris and around the world. From Provençal quilts to silk pajamas, via candlesticks, placemats, and blown glassware, Sophie pays vibrant tribute to the region where she has her roots. "From tableware to clothing, with Le Château de Ma Mère she offers a fresh vision of Provence," says Mathilde.

FACING PAGE, ABOVE, AND RIGHT
In her boutique, Le Château de Ma Mère on Rue de Grenelle, Sophie displays her collections of clothes and accessories, which borrow their manufacturing secrets from the finest Provençal artists and artisans.

Parisians

"Being a Parisian is not about being born in Paris, it's about being reborn there." – Sacha Guitry

PAGE 116
A boy with a boat on the Grand Bassin in the Jardin du Luxembourg.

PAGE 117
Minda the concierge, Mathilde, and Général the King Charles spaniel.

BELOW
Lena at the angle of Place Vendôme.

FACING PAGE
Lena in the Dior Haute Couture ateliers, during filming for a story with *Vogue Paris*.

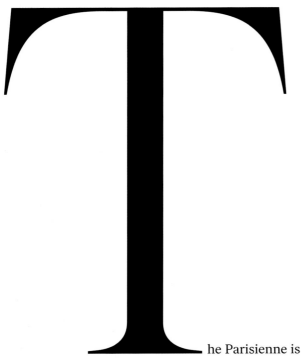

The Parisienne is the stuff of legend. Celebrated the world over, envied for her style, elegance, nonchalance, insouciance, and spontaneity, she is also charming and cheerful. She is unique.

Rousseau captured her in *Julie, or The New Héloïse* (the eighteenth century's bestseller) and she has been idolized ever since, especially for her innate bond with fashion. Legend has it that she never puts on weight, never shows her age, can throw on any old thing and look great, and her makeup is barely there. Plus she is a fund of good conversation, for was Paris not the birthplace of the literary salon?

But although she may look *au naturel*, the Parisienne is in fact a rigidly disciplined perfectionist. Don't be taken in: the way she looks, like everything else about her, is the product of sheer hard work and stubborn application.

Some of those here, like Mathilde, were born and brought up in the City of Light, others have made it their home. All have found love and success here. And all combine fulfilling professional lives with successful private lives in their chosen city.

Lena Situations

Lena Mahfouf rose to fame with her YouTube channel, where since 2017 this French-Algerian influencer has been sharing fashion tips and positivity, all in her own unique style, laced with wicked humor and an infectious sense of fun.

As well as being an influencer and content creator, she is also a successful author: the book she published in 2020 topped the book charts for weeks, rivaling the sales figures usually notched up by Prix Goncourt winners. She has twice been on the cover of *Elle* and has been featured in the *New York Times*, and she tries to share every side of herself, including her imperfections, with her millions of followers on social media. Her goal is to share the kindness and naturalness she advocates with an online community that values them too.

Sofia Achaval de Montaigu

Born in Buenos Aires, Sofia arrived in France at the beginning of the 2000s to attend Studio Berçot, the leading fashion school. During her time there she also worked as a model, and after graduation she became Vanessa Seward's assistant at Azzaro. After a time as fashion editor-at-large for *V Magazine*, she launched her Àcheval label in 2018.

Inspired by a mix of the cowboy style of Argentinian gauchos and 1970s fashion, her designs combine the masculine with the feminine, with boots, hats, and pants ever-present features.

In 2009, she married the writer Thibault de Montaigu, descended from the Gallimard family, French publishing aristocracy. They live in the heart of Saint-Germain-des-Prés with their two children, aged fourteen and eight. Mathilde: "She's delightful, hugely inspiring, and always one step ahead of the latest fashion."

RIGHT
Sofia in the Dior showroom, dressed for the catwalk show.

Francis Kurkdjian

Francis Kurkdjian found fame at the age of twenty-five with his creation of Le Mâle cologne for Jean Paul Gaultier. In 2009, he founded his own perfume house, attracting a discerning clientele with his fragrances. In 2021, he saw his dream of joining an haute couture house come true when he became Perfume Creation Director for Parfums Dior. He brings a modern touch to the house fragrances, while at the same time respecting their history.

Mathilde: "I met Francis when he arrived at Dior. He managed to make me change my perfume—I'd always worn Fracas by Piguet—by creating a sublime Tubérose for me, which as the name suggests is made from tuberose and roses. He also detected that I had a highly developed sense of smell and could have had a career as a nose, which I would have loved!"

RIGHT
Francis in his office, against an imposing backdrop of the high-rise buildings of La Défense.

Emmanuelle Alt

Her look and her style made her the perfect ambassador for *Vogue Paris*, for which she worked for twenty years and became the last editor-in-chief (it has now become *Vogue France*), making it more inclusive and ushering it into the digital age. Now a highly sought-after stylist and consultant, she is the epitome of Parisian style.

Born in Paris, she went to the same school as Mathilde, who remembers: "She was the first to have a car—we were so jealous!"

With the change in her professional life, Emmanuelle and her husband, the prominent creative director Franck Durand, left the 16th arrondissement and the house where they raised their two children to settle in the heart of the 6th arrondissement, overlooking the Palais du Luxembourg.

FACING PAGE
Emmanuelle entertains
in her kitchen; its
rustic spirit has been
intentionally retained.

BELOW
The salon windows
offer a breathtaking view
over the courtyard side of
the Palais du Luxembourg.

Tatiana de Nicolay

An illustrator and watercolorist based in Paris, Tatiana
has been a globetrotter since her early childhood
in a small village in Poland. She has studied calligraphy
in Cairo, economics in Brussels, design in Florence,
and embroidery in Paris and India. Trained at Jean Paul
Gaultier and Manish Arora, she has designed for the cult
magazine *Cabana* and has created interior and decorative
objets in partnership with Diptyque and Carolina Irving
& Daughters, among others, as well under her own label.

    Mathilde: "She has impeccable manners, among
the best in Paris: she'll send a handwritten note—in green
ink and beautiful handwriting—to thank you for
an invitation to a fashion show."

FACING PAGE AND LEFT
Exotic motifs from
Tatiana's watercolors.
ABOVE
Tatiana at home with
Mathilde, wearing
one of her robes that she
likes to wear as a coat.

Carla Bruni

Carla Bruni-Sarkozy needs no introduction. Born into
a family of wealthy industrialists who left Turin for Paris
in the early 1970s to escape the Red Brigades, she went
on to become a supermodel and later a singer-songwriter.
She adopted the language of Molière as her own, and her
first album, *Quelqu'un m'a dit*, sold over two million
copies. In marrying Nicolas Sarkozy in 2008 she
embraced the role of French First Lady, in which she
showed an unrivaled ability to embody Parisian elegance
on state visits.

Mathilde met her on a beach at Cap Nègre, where
they both had vacation homes. Then she met her again
on Rue Octave-Feuillet, where they were neighbors once
more. As teenagers they both caught the 63 bus to its
terminus at Porte de la Muette. "Life has always thrown
us together. I love her tremendous intelligence," Mathilde
concludes, "her great simplicity, and her loyalty."

LEFT
Xavier Niel with students
at École 42, which stays
open 24/7, every day
of the week.

Xavier Niel

A serial disrupter and internet pioneer in France, Xavier is the founder of Free. The first to offer telephone, television, and internet via a single box, he is constantly introducing improvements for mobile users. While chairing the board of Free (Iliad Group) is his core role, his other activities are no less exciting. As an investor he has always been a visionary, helping new start-ups to emerge. He's also a media entrepreneur, with a controlling stake in the major French daily *Le Monde* and a string of current affairs magazines. In 2017, he launched Station F, a business incubator offering specialist support service for start-ups. But it was at École 42 that he wanted to be photographed. Founded in 2013 by Xavier, École 42 is tuition-free, open 24/7, 365 days a year, and offers the best in computer science training. Its motto could be "Anyone, whatever their age or background, can learn to code and make a career of it." Ten years on, the school has seven campuses in France and forty-three partner campuses in twenty-nine countries.

Mathilde: "Xavier is the friend you dream of having. He's one of the most dependable people I know—a rare thing for someone who has so little time for himself. He's a visionary who is deeply human, with feet and heart firmly grounded."

134.

Natalia Vodianova

Her life is a modern fairy tale: supermodel, mother, wife, philanthropist, entrepreneur, Natalia was born in Gorky—Russia's fourth largest city, now Nizhny Novgorod—and grew up in a single-parent family with two younger sisters, one of whom was born with severe autism. As a teenager, she helped her mother on her fruit and vegetable stall in markets where temperatures often dropped to twenty degrees below zero. At the age of just fifteen, she set up her own fruit and vegetable business and then enrolled in a modeling agency, before leaving for Paris at seventeen, armed only with the English she had learned in three months. She then signed with Viva, a very Parisian agency that still looks after her to this day, and the rest is history. The greatest photographers, including Paolo Roversi, Mert & Marcus, and Mario Testino now compete to photograph her, and she is constantly booked for runway shows, magazine covers, and advertising campaigns. In 2004, she set up the Naked Heart Foundation, dedicated to combating the neglect of children with special needs, and to creating parks and playgrounds accessible to all children, regardless of their abilities.

Still actively involved in her foundation, she lives in Paris with her husband, Antoine Arnault, their two sons, and three children from her first marriage. Deeply devout, she chose to be photographed outside one of her favorite places, Alexander Nevsky Cathedral, known by Parisians as "the Russian church on Rue Daru."

FACING PAGE
The magnificently decorated dome of Alexander Nevsky Cathedral.

INSET
Engraving by Charles-Claude Bachelier of Alexander Nevsky Cathedral, the Russian Orthodox church on Rue Daru in the 8th arrondissement of Paris, consecrated in 1861.

RIGHT
Natalia on the steps of Alexander Nevsky Cathedral, the first Russian Orthodox church in Paris.

Antoine de Caunes

A multi-talented television personality, whose talent
lit up the glory years of Canal+ and who initiated
many shows about rock, Antoine de Caunes holds
the record for presenting the most César Awards
ceremonies, as well as being a radio presenter, actor,
and author. He and his wife, the journalist Daphné
Roulier, make an inspiring couple whose good looks
seem to defy the effects of time.

Maria de la Orden

A native of Madrid, Maria arrived in Paris ten years ago to pursue her law studies, living in a tiny studio in the Odéon neighborhood. Since then, she has launched her own label, cofounded La Veste with Blanca Miró, and married a prominent French industrialist.

During the Covid-19 pandemic, Maria managed to rally a community around her label, which was chic, fresh, and had a retro charm. Building on its early online success, she opened her first boutique on Rue de l'Université, a stone's throw from the Faubourg Saint-Germain.

She adores dinners with a theme, and is a superb hostess in her Directory-style home, with flowers on every table and beautifully chosen tableware, often vintage. The gentle fragrance of scented candles wafts through the reception rooms where she likes to gather her friends, young women who are as kind as they are elegant—new romantics of whom Maria is the leading light.

ABOVE
Maria in her boutique
on Rue de l'Université.
RIGHT
In her Directory-style
home, Maria has
become the most Parisian
of Madrid natives.
FACING PAGE
A "New Romantics"
get-together at Maria's.

Julie de Libran

Born in Provence, Julie grew up in California, where she dreamed of fashion and Paris as she leafed through her mother's copies of *Vogue Paris*. She was already designing her own clothes and personalizing bought ones. Encouraged by her parents to study fashion seriously, she enrolled in the Istituto Marangoni in Milan. After graduating, she worked with some of the greatest names in fashion: Gianni Versace, Gianfranco Ferré, Miuccia Prada, and Marc Jacobs.

After taking over as artistic director of Sonia Rykiel in 2014, she set up her own fashion house in 2019, with a philosophy that perfectly reflects her lifestyle choices—cycling everywhere and eating organic vegetables from her garden in the country. She makes her ready-to-wear designs and jewelry in very small quantities, often working with offcuts, so that her pieces are by their very nature produced in very limited, numbered editions. When the fabric runs out, they are definitively sold out and can never be made again.

At her home in the 6th arrondissement—a former warehouse transformed by interior designer Charles Zana into a country house in the heart of the city, flanked by two green spaces designed by Louis Benech—she organizes fashion shows for her collections and keeps open house for her designer friends. In July 2023, it was her friends' daughters who modeled her haute couture collection, in line with the philosophy of a designer who wants her dresses to be handed down. Immune to passing trends, she creates fashion that is timeless.

Mathilde and Julie met while working at Prada. "Julie designs for women who work. She's brilliant at designing mismatched clothes and keeping them fresh."

Julie: "Paris was my dream! I love everything in Paris!"

"What's wonderful about Paris is that you can have a packed cultural and social life while also taking time out for yourself and your family."

142.

RIGHT
A bench by the artist
Latifa Echakhch in the
entrance hall to Julie's
house, with a curving
stair rail designed
and made by her cousin,
the animal sculptor
and painter Aurélien
Raynaud.

Porthault

Founded over a century ago, Porthault is a byword for the finest in household linens. Since becoming the first to dare to offer printed bed linen, they have never ceased to innovate, with ranges of table linens, towels, and bedding for cribs. Porthault applies their famous heart motif (a favorite of the Duchess of Windsor) or shamrock motif (a tribute to Louise de Vilmorin) to the finest-quality cottons. Their client list is a journey through history, from Charles de Gaulle to Winston Churchill, from Jackie Kennedy to Gabrielle Chanel, and from Audrey Hepburn to Grace Kelly.

Mathilde: "For school trips to the seaside, my mother used to pack Porthault sheets and towels in our bags. We were horribly embarrassed in front of our classmates, and we envied them their sleeping bags!"

LEFT
Sophie Fontanel in beautiful lucky sheets. "When I was young I didn't have a bean, so I would go to Porthault and buy just the washcloths. Part of my Armenian family came from Turkey, and from grandparents down to children we became integrated through a taste for beauty and refinement that we shared with French people and with Paris.

When I go into a Paris apartment and see a bath towel with a floral motif in the bathroom, I feel straight away that I'm part of a story. The long history of the love of elegance. At least, I hope so!"

ABOVE
A decorative corner in the Porthault boutique on Avenue Marceau, in the 16th arrondissement.

LEFT AND BELOW
Breakfast in Chloé's
garden and her work *Heart*,
inspired by pop culture.
FACING PAGE
Chloé with one
of her creations.

146.

Chloé Bolloré

Sunny in temperament and always good-humored, Chloé is an accomplished artist, wife, and mother. A lifelong fan of pop art, she took the plunge in 2013, initially creating digital works. They were an immediate success. She has since expanded her repertoire with message mirrors and 3D cut-metal sculptures, all homages to icons of popular culture.

Born into the Bouygues engineering family, Chloé married into another major French company, and now lives in a leafy setting in Paris with her husband, Yannick Bolloré, and their four daughters.

"Underneath that light-hearted exterior, Chloé and I always have deep conversations," says Mathilde. "She's a woman of great enthusiasm, who listens and never judges. She's also an exceptional mother."

148.

Morin Oluwole

The Global Director of Luxury for Meta was born in Nigeria, which she left at the age of fifteen for the United States, and she is now in love with Paris. Morin joined Facebook in 2006, after studying at Stanford. Passionate about fashion and lifestyle, she moved to Paris in 2015, with a plan to persuade luxury brands to join the social network created by Mark Zuckerberg as well as Instagram, the favorite platform for influencers. Arriving without a word of French or any familiarity with Parisian ways, she lost no time in bringing herself up to speed, and was soon speaking flawless French and mastering all the unwritten codes of life in Paris. And by 2017, Louis Vuitton runway shows were live on Instagram!

Morin Oluwole: "I became the woman I am in Paris, through the joys and the more difficult moments, until I found everlasting love. Paris will forever be a part of my life."

Mathilde: "She's a visionary, an entrepreneur with a deep love of Paris and France."

Ondine Saglio

The daughter of Valérie Schlumberger, a French pioneer in ethical and fair trade, Ondine
has taken over the running of CSAO (Compagnie du Sénégal et de l'Afrique de l'Ouest),
the boutique-gallery specializing in African arts and crafts that was founded by
her mother. She has since added two embroidery workshops in Senegal and established
the Association du Sénégal et de l'Afrique de l'Ouest (ASAO). Parisians love her wax
or Liberty-print cushions with gold embroidery. Mathilde: "She brings Africa to us in Paris.
Deeply committed to craftsmanship and to supporting the women of Gorée through
her association, Ondine has a beautiful spirit."

**FACING PAGE, LEFT,
AND ABOVE**
Displays of colorful
carpets and African
artisan work in the CSAO
boutique-gallery
on Rue Elzévir, run
by Ondine.

Isabelle and Christine d'Ornano

Countess Isabelle d'Ornano and her daughter Christine are famous for their style: bold, original, colorful, and, above all, elegant. With Philippe, Isabelle's son and Christine's brother, they run Sisley, ensuring the success of this pioneering company in phyto-cosmetology. Offering products—skincare, fragrances, and makeup— that are largely made in France, this Paris-based family firm has enjoyed exceptional growth since it was founded in 1976. The company's values of creativity and authenticity have now gained a worldwide reputation, with each generation making its own contribution, keeping it contemporary without altering its DNA.

Mathilde: "With a cosmopolitan and international background, Isabelle d'Ornano has an enquiring mind and is a patron of the arts, and her daughter is following in her footsteps."

Isabelle d'Ornano: "Paris is the tradition of savoir-faire in the worlds of fashion and beauty. Luxury lives in Paris, and Paris must champion its luxury and *art de vivre*. People love stories, and the luxury houses of Paris have some marvelous ones that are also true!"

RIGHT
Mother and daughter in the cabinet of curiosities that is Isabelle's office.

ABOVE
Jeanne in the street in
Paris, wearing a design
from her own label,
photographed
by Harry Gruyaert.

RIGHT AND FACING PAGE, TOP
A quintessential Parisienne
who values all that is
authentic, Jeanne chose
Aux Crus de Bourgogne
on Rue Bachaumont
for the launch
of her cosmetics line,
Les Filles en Rouje.

FACING PAGE, BOTTOM
Jeanne in her office,
photographed
by Vincent Ferrané.

PAGES 156–157
The façades of
seventeenth-century
Parisian house,
with the imposing
church of Saint-Gervais
behind them.

Jeanne Damas

A Parisienne to her fingertips—her parents ran a café-restaurant not far from Place de la Bastille—Jeanne is a muse, model, and fashion designer with millions of subscribers, who launched Rouje in 2016. The clothing label, which offers clothes that are sexy, fresh, and immaculately cut, immediately achieved a highly covetable status among her large community of followers. Building on this success, Jeanne added a skincare line, which she was very soon selling worldwide.

For Jeanne, "The Parisienne doesn't exist. There are as many Parisiennes as there are women in Paris. The only true Parisienne is Paris itself."

Mathilde: "This lovely young woman, now an international success, helps out in a soup kitchen at Christmas. Which perfectly sums up the kind of person she is."

C'est si *Bon*

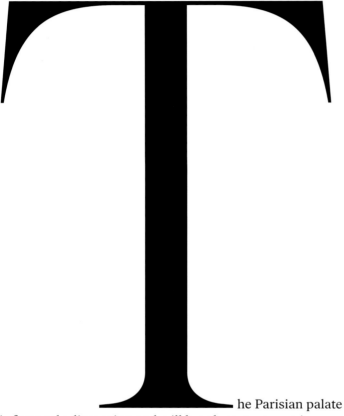

T he Parisian palate is famously discerning and will brook no compromise. From Michelin-starred restaurants to market stalls, from *salons de thé* to inspired local bistros, the City of Light invites you to indulge in the pleasures of the table.

It was Paris that witnessed the birth of a concept that was subsequently to spread to every city throughout the world: the restaurant.

In 1765, Mathurin Roze de Chantoiseau—not a restaurateur but a philanthropist and economist—wanted to make good food accessible to as many people as possible. At the time, the only places to eat out were insalubrious inns, with set menus served at fixed times and at prices based on the "look of the customer." Roze de Chantoiseau opened an establishment that was clean, where customers could sit at separate tables and choose dishes from a menu that displayed the prices. The restaurant as we still know it today was born.

Paris is the place where chefs from around the world choose to train, a place that recognizes and encourages the most talented. The city also offers the best food shops in the world, and with 1,180 boulangeries, a baguette is never more than a five-minute walk away!

Le Voltaire

Set in the house in which the famous writer and philosopher died, Le Voltaire is a classic, popular with the fashion world and members of the Académie Française alike. Here Thierry (known as "Titi") pampers his regular clientele, remembering their names and preferred tables and even their favorite dishes. The cuisine is French, delicious and generous, served in a setting that is as warm as it is chic.

The iconic dish at Le Voltaire is *œuf mayonnaise* "James," named for James Lord, an American soldier who arrived in Paris at the Liberation and whose favorite dish it was, and still priced at just 90 centimes (just under one US dollar). A regular who never left the neighborhood, he was painted by Giacometti and wrote acclaimed biographies of Giacometti and Picasso and Dora Maar.

Coming to Le Voltaire is to experience a menu and an atmosphere that are reassuringly unchanged.

Mathilde: "Whenever we go to Le Voltaire, Thierry and Richard are waiting to greet us. At Le Voltaire you're dining out but you feel like you're at home."

La Poule au Pot

Élodie and Jean-François Piège bought this Paris institution in 2018. Their cuisine, of traditional bourgeois inspiration, is complemented by a well-researched wine list. A journey to the heart of France's culinary heritage offers *escargots en coquille*, an exceptional *hachis parentier*, and, of course, *poule au pot*: mouthwatering, quintessentially French dishes served in a setting that has been refreshed without losing its original character.

Mathilde with three of her favorite chefs

From left to right: Jean-François Piège, who with his wife, Élodie, owns not only Poule au Pot, but also the Clover Grill and the Grand Restaurant, awarded two Michelin stars.

Alain Passard, king and virtuoso chef of seasonal vegetables, holder of three Michelin stars since 1996.

Jean Imbert, a youthful forty-something who says he owes it all to his grandmother and who has forged a meteoric career in just ten years. He now heads up iconic Paris dining spots including the Michelin-starred Jean Imbert au Plaza Athénée at the Hôtel Plaza Athénée, and Monsieur Dior, the first Dior restaurant.

ABOVE LEFT
A specialty of the
restaurant Monsieur Dior,
created by Jean Imbert.
ABOVE RIGHT
Jean-François Piège's
chic *pâté en croûte*.
LEFT
A dish created by Alain
Passard for his restaurant,
l'Arpège.

CRÈMERIE - FROMAGERIE

NE PAS
TOUCHER
NE PAS SENTIR
LES AROMATES
Merci

Butternut
3,99€ kg
ESPAGNE

SALADE
1€ 20

CHOU FLEUR

Confiture maison
-Coings -Nectarines
-Fraises -Abricots
-Oranges
10€

The President Wilson Market

Twice a week, on Wednesday and Saturday, Avenue du Président-Wilson hosts one of the best of all Paris markets, an epicurean culinary promenade flanked by amazing museums: the Musée Guimet, Palais Galliera, the Musée d'Art Moderne, and the Palais de Tokyo. A favorite with Michelin-starred chefs, the market brings together organic growers and smallholders, excellent fishmongers and charcutiers, as well as dishes from around the world to take away.

Caractère de Cochon

It's the first store of its kind in Paris, dedicated to hams and charcuterie. Opened by Solo Raveloson, it offers a wide range of cured meats, a selection of the finest products from non-industrialized farms throughout Europe, including Spain, Hungary, and Italy. It also offers pâtés and terrines, as well as wines and cheeses.

Pure temptation is available in the form of your own customized ham sandwich, for which you can choose your ham—Tuscan with pepper, *Iberico Cebo de Campo*, Burgundian *jambon persillé*, hay-smoked from the Vosges, Provençal with rosemary—and your butter, whether unsalted, semi-salted, or salted. Mathilde gives in to temptation: "It's impossible to resist!"

PAGES 168–169
Saint-Paul-Saint-Louis church in the Saint-Paul district and rattan chairs, typical of Parisian terraces.

LEFT, RIGHT AND FACING PAGE
Why not give the lunchtime crowds a miss and head to this unique store on Rue Charlot in the Marais for its delectable sandwiches?

ABOVE
One of the most beautifull doors in Paris, photographed in the Marais district.

PAGES 172–173
Two very Parisian spots around the Palais Royal: the Café de l'Époque, a timeless brasserie, and Le Grand Véfour, a jewel of eighteenth-century decorative art and a high temple of French gastronomy.

170.

RIGHT
Isabella Capece's indulgent
vegan lemon cheesecake.
FACING PAGE
Mathilde in the doorway
of Maisie Café on Rue du
Mont-Thabor, with Isabella
Capece, Mélanie Huynh,
Luiz Broetto, and
Alexandra Golovanoff.

Maisie Café

In just a few years, this Rue du Mont-Thabor address has become an unmissable
spot for vegans and a standard-bearer for the art of health-conscious living.

Opened in 2016 by Isabella Capece and her husband, Xavier Barroux,
with a view to sharing Isabella's wellness lifestyle, the café makes daily deliveries
all over Paris and is busy all day, from breakfast to teatime.

Xavier has made it his core business, while Isabella—who is also a PR
executive advising both brands and institutions—is responsible for the philosophy,
development, and public relations of this uniquely atmospheric spot.

RIGHT
Her office is upstairs, but
Apollonia is often to be
found in the shop, to which
tourists and regulars flock.
Every day, seventy of
the large round loaves
called *miches* emerge from
this oven.

Poilâne

Their bread is distributed worldwide, but Apollonia
Poilâne is pictured here at the historic bakery founded
by her grandfather in 1932 on Rue du Cherche-Midi,
in the heart of the 6th arrondissement.

   Following the sudden death of her father,
Lionel, in 2002, Apollonia found herself at the head
of the family business at the age of just eighteen.
So she carried on the work that her parents
had started: turning their neighborhood bakery
into a business of international renown.

   While their bread and cookies are available
throughout the world, only the five Parisian
boulangeries offer their famous *tarte aux pommes*,
flan, and *pain d'épices*.

Barthélémy

Nicole Barthélémy may have passed the baton to a new owner, but the cheeses in this temple to the art of cheesemaking remain as outstanding as ever. The legendary store on Rue de Grenelle, which for decades has supplied the cheese boards of French presidents and so many others, has kept its original décor of marble shelves and ceramic tiles. Here customers can choose between a universally acclaimed Fontainebleau, goats' cheeses in every shade of white, an earthy Saint-Nectaire, crumbly Cantals and Salers, creamy Reblochon, perfectly ripe Camemberts, creamy Bries, and Saint-Marcellins that are smooth but not runny, all matured on site in the store's cellars.

Mathilde: "Cheese and dairy are my guilty pleasures—I have to discipline myself not to eat them too often, so when I transgress I go to Barthélémy. I'll come home with a Brillat-Savarin, an extra-mature Mimolette, some Fontainebleau, and some salted butter sold by weight."

LEFT, ABOVE, AND FACING PAGE
The finest cheeses have ripened in this temple of ceramic tiles and marble since 1971.
INSET
At Parisian dinner parties, personalized Poilâne rolls serve as place-markers for guests.

178.

Le Relais de L'Entrecôte

The winning formula here was invented by Paul Gineste de Saurs in 1959: a fixed menu and no reservations, meaning long lines for every service for over half a century. Unheard of in Paris. The founder's daughters now share four Paris venues between them, one looking after Marbeuf, Saint-Benoît, and Montparnasse, and the other Porte Maillot.

Customers can enjoy generous portions of *salade aux noix*, *contre-filet de bœuf* with a delectable sauce whose recipe is "a state secret," homemade fries, and wonderful desserts. All this is served in a welcoming setting of wood paneling, mirrors, and vintage posters, by friendly waitresses in impeccable black uniforms with white collars and aprons. Despite the crowds of tourists, it has managed to remain authentically Parisian.

Mathilde: "We used to go there as children, it was our French McDonald's. The sauce is impossible to resist. My son Carlo, who lives abroad, always takes me there when he's in Paris."

FACING PAGE AND RIGHT
Mathilde with her son,
Carlo Agostinelli.
INSET
Delicious fries from
Le Relais de l'Entrecôte.
PAGES 182–183
The Place des Vosges
and its arcades.
In the center, a map of
Paris with its monuments,
dating from 1930.

Maison Louis Fouquet

This confectioner and chocolatier established under the Second Empire boasts a highly exclusive clientele. In its 172 years of existence, its historic premises on Rue Laffitte and Rue François 1er have welcomed Claude Monet, Christian Dior, Gertrude Stein, and Yves Saint Laurent. The characteristic brown bag with its distinctive typography holds out a promise of delights within.

Mathilde lists just some of them: "Salted butter caramels in buttered wrappers. Bonbons and chocolates in glass jars: ideal, ultra-chic gifts for weekends with friends. The only mustard pots you can leave on the table. The green and white after-dinner mints that Jacqueline de Ribes always serves her guests."

ABOVE, RIGHT, AND FACING PAGE
The historic store on Rue Laffitte, one of the oldest *chocolateries* in Paris.

Carette

Early in the morning, its terrace with views of the Trocadero and the Eiffel Tower is magical. Carette was part of Mathilde's childhood, her salon de thé on Place du Trocadéro, just a stone's throw from her grandmother's apartment, where she would go for lunch on Wednesdays. Madame Carette still presided over the cash register in those days, in the original art deco interior—it opened in 1927—which has survived to this day. Mathilde: "Now a victim of its own success, Carette is slightly overrun by tourists, but I still go there for their little cucumber, tomato, and egg sandwiches, and I can't resist their best macaron made with real bitter chocolate."

FACING PAGE AND LEFT
Mathilde still regularly stops at Carette to enjoy her favorite sandwiches and the unbeatable view of Place du Trocadéro.

Paris *in Bloom*

I

n Paris, flowers are everywhere, adorning the façade of an Haussmann apartment building, like the wisteria we wait to see in flower every year, in window boxes, and in gardens. Paris invented the modern bouquet. As with fashion and food, it is in Paris that flower arrangements are constantly being given a new twist.

There are nearly five hundred florists in Paris, 425 to be precise. Each has its own special flower, style, and clientele, whether from the neighborhood, or further afield. Mostly committed to keeping things local, these florists devote the same passion to every occasion, big or small. Lining the sidewalks with their charming, informal bouquets, they fill the streets with color and add that joyful, chic touch that is the hallmark of Paris.

PAGES 188–189
The charm of Parisian façades full of flowers.
ABOVE
An arrangement by Castor Fleuriste in a vase by Mathilde Martin.
FACING PAGE
A floral composition on the staircase of the legendary Christian Dior *hôtel particulier* at 30 Avenue Montaigne, created by Éric Chauvin in 2018 and photographed by Raphaël Dautigny.

Éric Chauvin

Established in Paris in 2000, this son of a farmer creates fabulous décors with flowers, whether lining the walls at Raf Simons's first couture show for Dior with a million blooms or transforming the Grand Staircase at the Opéra Garnier with a floral installation. He supplies flowers to hostesses who are as exacting as they are influential, composing bouquets with his unique poetic touch. His reputation has long since spread beyond Paris and he works all over the world, but he always returns to his native Perche region and to his historic address on Rue Jean-Nicot, in the heart of the 7th arrondissement.

A Parisian bouquet, he says, is "an armful of garden roses, flowers that you love in the country and long for in the city. A bouquet for the Parisienne who loves the simple things in life."

Mathilde on Éric: "An exquisite young man whom I met when I arrived at Dior. He dresses my dinner parties with seasonal flowers, and I give them to my guests when they leave. I can't bear to see flowers die."

FACING PAGE AND BELOW
The front of Chauvin's
boutique, with Éric
photographed among
his flowers.

"As with fashion and food, it is in Paris that flower arrangements are constantly being given a new twist."

194.

Lachaume Paris

This prestigious name has been supplying the highest echelons of Parisian society since 1845. A few years ago, sisters Stéphanie Primet and Caroline Cnocquaert took over the running of this Paris institution, bought by their grandmother Giuseppina Callegari in 1970.

Today they have pushed its boundaries beyond France, with commissions that are ever more extravagant. From a bouquet delivered to a London hotel for the fiftieth birthday of a beloved wife, to a semi-trailer filled with flowers to recreate Maxim's in a Gstaad chalet, nothing is too much for them, true to the Lachaume motto: "Never refuse an order." The love of flowers is a family trait. "It was in the old Les Halles in Paris that our parents first met. Our grandmother soon realized why her son was ordering more and more lilies: Maman was the grower's daughter. Our younger sister is a landscape gardener."

For Mathilde, Lachaume is an institution. "To receive a bouquet from Lachaume is to fall in love with the person who sent it."

Moulié Paris

A pair of standard camellias nearly twelve feet (3.5m) tall flank
the entrance to this unmissable florist, a family business since 1870:
the Lange family, then the Savart family, and, in 1978, the Moulié
family, when two young employees, Henri and Dominique Moulié,
took it over at the end of their apprenticeship. With its position
on the majestic and discreet Place du Palais Bourbon, it became
a destination.

It is their sons, Julien and Thomas, who now continue this
adventure, preferring to keep things in house and sourcing from only
the best producers. They supply flowers to major fashion houses,
their artistic directors, and numerous politicians. But, as with all
florists, their discretion is legendary.

Mathilde praises Moulié: "For Julien, and because the way Moulié
decorates the Place du Palais Bourbon with flowers is enchanting.
And for their Papa Meilland roses, with their intoxicating perfume,
lemony and floral, and their magnificent deep crimson blooms."

City of Culture

Liya Kebede

Ethiopian by birth, Liya spends most of the year in Paris. She has had an uninterrupted career as a top model since she was eighteen, and became a mother at twenty-two and a UN ambassador at twenty-seven. Two years later she became an entrepreneur, launching Lemlem, a sustainable, artisan-driven label that provides jobs for women in Addis Ababa. Those who know her know that she always has a book to hand. "Books have been my companions, my friends, my therapists," she sums up. For the launch of her book bags, she chose Maison Fleuret on Rue des Saints-Pères, a delightful space with book-lined walls and delicious cappuccinos and cookies, a dream spot for reading and sharing, much-loved for its brunches. A book to read in Paris? *Giovanni's Room* by James Baldwin. When his fiancée leaves for Spain and the United States, David, a young American, is left alone in Paris. There he falls in love with a bartender, Giovanni. Published in 1956, the novel has become a classic, a deeply moving and troubling study of sexual identity, the clash of cultures, and the nature of love.

T

he undisputed capital of culture and the arts, Paris embraces, inspires, and encourages art in all its forms. Its countless bookstores, galleries, art fairs, and salons presenting the work of artists every year, both established and up and coming, make Paris an unmissable destination for aficionados of beauty in all its forms.

Since the nineteenth century, Paris has been a place of refuge and freedom for painters, writers, and musicians from all over the world, who have come to breathe the air of liberty that reigns in the City of Light. After the artists of Romanticism flocked to the Nouvelle Athènes district in the nineteenth century, three other districts succeeded each other as epicenters of the world's cultural life: Montmartre, where Degas, Matisse, Toulouse-Lautrec, and Renoir lived before World War I; Montparnasse, chosen by Picasso, Modigliani, Man Ray, Hemingway, and Foujita in the Roaring Twenties; and Saint-Germain-des-Prés, home to France's leading publishing houses, with many of their authors nearby. At the tables of Café de Flore, Brasserie Lipp, or Les Deux Magots, Simone de Beauvoir and Jean-Paul Sartre, Boris Vian and Samuel Beckett pondered the world, while the neighboring cellar bars echoed to the first notes of jazz to be played in Europe. Paris offers a cultural life that is rich, intense, and of a quality that is the envy of many. Here Mathilde introduces us to the places and people she loves.

The Bouquinistes

A stroll along the Seine is also an opportunity to rummage for treasures among the bouquinistes. Selling vintage and antiquarian books, magazines, and prints, the nine hundred book boxes perched along the stone parapet are a quintessentially Parisian image.

PAGES 202–203
Bouquiniste boxes
photographed near
the Pont Neuf.
RIGHT
The booksellers at
Galignani are always ready
and willing to find you
the book of your dreams.
Danielle Cillien Sabatier
breathes dynamism
and fun into this Paris
institution.

Galignani

Established at this address since 1856 (after
Giovanni Antonio Galignani first set up shop
on Rue Vivienne in 1801) and specializing
in books in English, this is not only the oldest
Franco-English bookshop in continental
Europe, but also the most beautiful and
best-stocked bookshop in Paris. And not just
books in English, but also an outstanding
department of works on the fine arts, fashion,
and interior design, first set up during the
wartime Occupation when it was impossible
to obtain books from British and American
publishers.

The store is still owned by descendants
of Galignani. Danielle Cillien Sabatier,
general manager since 2009, has introduced
essential modern practices into the legendary
institution, while still preserving its
centuries-old heritage. With her ability to
select the finest art books, the most pertinent
biographies, and the most enthralling novels,
she extends a unique welcome, breathes life
into this celebration of books and culture,
and organizes regular book signings that
are also fascinating meetings with authors.

To go through the doors of 224 Rue
de Rivoli, opposite the Tuileries Gardens, is
to be enveloped by the aromas of wood and
books, to travel through time and space as
you browse the books on the shelves, to leaf
through the beautiful books on display and
benefit from the advice of expert booksellers.
Used to dealing with a clientele of hard-to-
please aesthetes from all over the world, they
invariably have intriguing recommendations
up their sleeves.

Mathilde: "It's a pleasure to be welcomed
here—they know who you are and what
you like, and their advice is always spot on."

Diana Widmaier Picasso

A granddaughter of Pablo Picasso—her mother, Maya, who passed away at the end of 2022, was his eldest daughter—Diana has many strings to her bow. After setting up Menē, a radical investment jewelry brand, listed on the stock exchange, selling 24-carat gold and platinum jewelry by weight, in 2023 she began work on the catalogue raisonné of Picasso's sculptures, as well as managing his personal collection. Art historian and exhibition curator, after specializing in old master drawings, her heritage has caught up with her and she now mounts magnificent exhibitions based around Picasso's work. Here she is photographed in the Hôtel Salé, a marvel of the baroque built in the heart of the Marais in the mid-seventeenth century, and since 1985 home to the Musée Picasso. Within these walls, well worth a visit for their architecture alone, lies the world's richest public collection of Picasso works, with no fewer than five thousand paintings, sculptures, ceramics, and tens of thousands of archive documents. Diana has a six-year-old daughter, Luna, who insisted on choosing her outfit for our photograph. Mathilde: "She has an amazing sense of humor, and she makes art history fascinating and fun."

LEFT AND ABOVE
The exterior of the Musée Picasso and the courtyard façade.
FACING PAGE
Diana, on a chair by Alberto Giacometti from his last commission, a set of fifty chairs, benches, lights, and tables designed exclusively for the museum in 1985.

Vanessa Seward
and Bertrand Burgalat

A couple for almost twenty years, they live
in a world of old-fashioned glamour. He is a
musician known for his multifaceted talents:
as an arranger, composer, producer, and singer,
he has produced albums by Valérie Lemercier
and Michel Houellebecq, contributed
to albums by Christophe Willem and Marc
Lavoine, and composed film scores and
numerous other pieces of music.

Mathilde has known Vanessa since they
were at school together. Born in Argentina,
she is nonetheless quintessentially Parisian.
Way back when she was an intern at Chanel
with Mathilde's Uncle Gilles, she was already
an inspiration. A stylist for many years,
she brought glamour back to Azzaro before
launching her own label, which Mathilde
still wears.

"Her designs make me feel I look good,
like a Parisienne. When we have lunch together
we're like two girlfriends straight out of a Kiraz
drawing. She's exquisite and has amazing style.
Nowadays she shows just as much talent
as a portrait painter—but I hope she never
stops making clothes."

Vanessa Seward

"If Paris was a sound?
'Sonal Roissy CDG,' composed by Bernard Parmegiani
in 1971 for Paris Charles de Gaulle airport.
If Paris was a painting?
Portrait of Sarah Bernhardt by Georges Clairin,
on display at the Petit Palais." – **Vanessa and Bertrand**

FACING PAGE
Self-portrait by Vanessa
Seward.

FAR LEFT AND LEFT
The singer and actress
Calypso Valois in front
of her portrait at Vanessa's
first private view, under
the arcades of the Palais
Royal in April 2023.

ABOVE
Mathilde with the jewelry
designer Elie Top,
under the arcades
of the Palais Royal.

Raphaëlla Riboud Seydoux and Alessandro Pron

La Galerie Italienne

When she met Alessandro, a Turin native and third-generation art and antique dealer, Raphaëlla, who had previously worked for Condé Nast and then Dior before launching her own chic homewear label, decided to join him in his Galerie Italienne venture. In this space of forty-eight hundred square feet (450 sq m), the couple—who have been married since 2018 and have had three daughters in three years—stage six annual exhibitions, to which they also add art fairs, creating a lively space around the artists they represent, who include Pietro Ruffo, Maurizio Donzelli, Giuseppe Gallo, and Alice Gavalet.

Mathilde: "Raphaëlla already had great style and an innate sense of observation when we met at Dior. She's a hard worker and that pays off. She and her husband have introduced me to young, affordable artists. I'm lucky to have their guidance."

City of Culture

LEFT
A dinner for L'Artisan
Parfumeur, organized
by Victoria's agency
in the workshop at
the Manufacture de Sèvres.
Mathilde: "Victoria has
a gift for finding original
venues for her dinners."

Victoria Botana de Beauvau

A discreet creative director and producer of bespoke events such as
weddings and anniversaries, Victoria has rapidly made a name for herself
in Paris for the unique quality and originality of the occasions she organizes.
Victoria is also the chatelaine of Haroué, the chateau with 365 windows that
has been dubbed the Chambord of Lorraine. Built by an ancestor in the early
eighteenth century, it has stayed in the family ever since. Victoria gained
experience at Dior and Hermès before setting up her own business.
Her apartment, with its breathtaking view of the basilica of Sainte-Clotilde,
is a stylish mix of family heirlooms and objets brought back from abroad.

Mathilde: "I lent her the dress she wore for her eighteenth birthday ball.
I worked with her at Dior. She influenced my decision to let my children
go to school in the UK. Victoria has become the person who organizes
the most beautiful dinners. Not only are they ravishingly pretty, but she
also pulls off the tour de force of making them fun and very laid back!
She's always one step ahead."

"I like to have lunch at Café Rhodia,
in the heart of the Musée Bourdelle, just behind
Montparnasse, a wonderful place that was
the studio and home of the sculptor
Antoine Bourdelle." – **Victoria**

Les puces

Covering seventeen acres (7 ha) at the gates of Paris and welcoming five million visitors a year, this cluster of fifteen flea markets is the largest vintage and antique market in the world.

The Marché Paul Bert-Serpette is where top interior designers head to hunt down treasures from seasoned dealers. For a few years it belonged to the Duke of Westminster—the sixth richest man in the UK at his death—before he sold it on in 2014.

A weekend trip *aux puces* is a typically Parisian activity. You always bump into someone you know, and Mathilde, who knows all its alleyways, is no exception.

FACING PAGE
The Olivier d'Ythurbide & Associé stand in the Marché Serpette offers vintage and antique furniture and objets d'art, with paintings from the sixteenth to the early twentieth century.

ABOVE
A market alleyway and a framing stand.

RIGHT
Hedi, the parking warden at the Marché Paul Bert-Serpette.

"My mother used to go there every Friday as the stalls were being set up, like a fishing expedition. She would always come back with something. She gave us the concept of objets that were charming but not necessarily expensive." – **Mathilde**

FACING PAGE AND ABOVE
Les Tables d'Eva's stand in the Marché Serpette, where Mathilde goes to hunt for vintage dinner services.
LEFT
One of the market alleys. Mathilde: "I never go to the flea market with anything specific. My motto is, 'I never need anything,' but I want everything!'"

Eva Jospin

Eva Jospin's remarkable landscapes in corrugated cardboard—a material that she says "helps us to give form to ideas"—transport us to worlds of the imagination and make her one of the most noticeable artists on the French contemporary art scene.

In her studio, cardboard is everywhere. Cutting, gluing, sanding, trimming, Eva and her team shape it into forests or architectural landscapes. This meticulous, painstaking, and repetitive process creates works of art that are profound and poetic, and that have already been acquired by many institutions and museums. Eva has created several scenographies for the Dior shows of Maria Grazia Chiuri, Artistic Director of women's collections at Dior, whose commitment to parity and respect for women she shares.

Eva: "Places in Paris that I like to show people: the Musée des Plans-reliefs, the military model museum in Les Invalides; the foyer of the Théâtre des Champs-Élysées, for its Vuillard paintings; the Musée de la Chasse et de la Nature, with artworks and taxidermy animals in two magnificent townhouses in the Marais, the seventeenth-century Hôtel de Guénégaud and the eighteenth-century Hôtel de Mongelas (including one of my works on permanent exhibition); and the grotto in the Parc des Buttes-Chaumont, built in a former gypsum quarry and created, like the rest of the park, for the 1867 Universal Exhibition (and impossibly romantic.)"

Marie Victoire Poliakoff and Sacha Floch Poliakoff

A passion for painting runs in the blood of this mother and daughter who both live in Saint-Germain-des-Prés. In her apartment, Marie Victoire, gallerist and granddaughter of the artist Serge Poliakoff, keeps Russian traditions alive. Several of her grandfather's paintings hang on the walls, alongside others by her daughter Sacha and the artists she has supported for over thirty years in her Galerie Pixi on Rue de Seine, where she exhibits works by artists including Duncan Hannah, Elizabeth Lennard, and Denis Polge.

Sacha, whose charming apartment is under the eaves, is an illustrator and painter who is also the daughter of the illustrator and comic-book artist Floch (who signs his work Floc'h). Following the major success of her first exhibitions, the young artist is forging her reputation with works imbued with nostalgia and a very personal style.

Mathilde: "I met Marie Victoire when I was working at *Glamour*. I'm moved by their Slavic sensibilities. They both have exquisite taste."

ABOVE, RIGHT, AND FACING PAGE
Marie Victoire at home, with her daughter, Sacha, and her dog, Molly. On the table, a delicious coulibiac from Bread & Roses.

LEFT
In Sacha's apartment,
an irresistible table
setting is surrounded by
her inspired paintings.
ABOVE
Sacha photographed
in her painter's apron.

On with the Show!

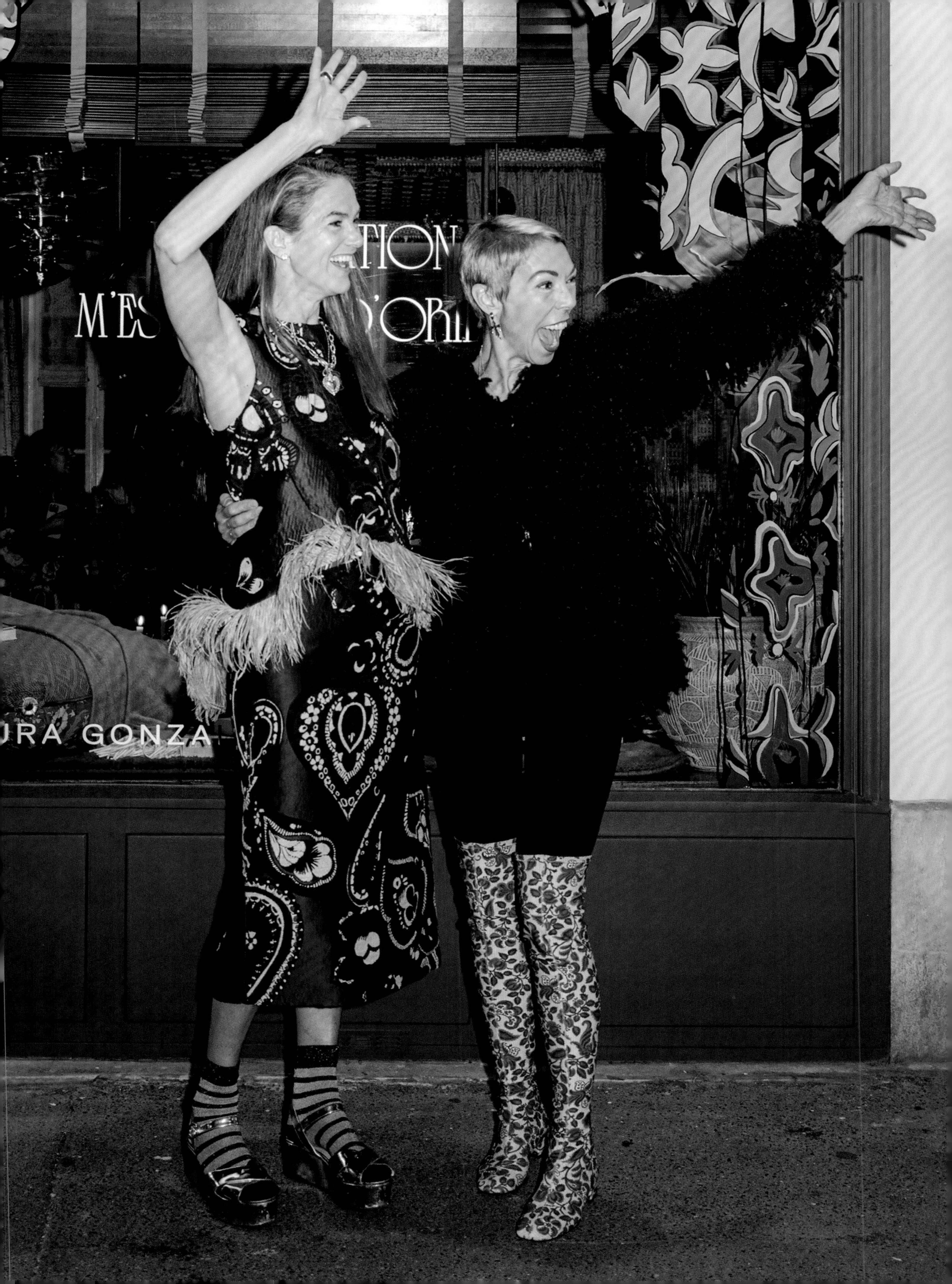
ATION
M'ES
D'ORI
URA GONZA

P aris is the art of performance. On any Saturday evening in Paris, you can see three hundred and fifty films or go to three hundred shows or sixty-two concerts.

Parisians' love of going out has a long history. As early as 1744, an almanac was published listing the programs of the capital's theaters, including the Comédie Française and the Opéra Comique, along with anecdotes about the playwrights and actors. Nowadays, Paris boasts one hundred and thirty theaters, including the world's smallest (La Petite Loge, seating twenty-five), examples from the eighteenth century, such as the Théâtre du Palais Royal, and the nineteenth, such as the Théâtre du Gymnase, and wonderful art deco buildings, such as the Théâtre des Champs Élysées and the Folies Bergère. Together they symbolize the richness and variety of cultural life of Paris.

It was in Paris, on December 28, 1895, that the Lumière brothers organized the first screening to a paying public in the history of cinema, with a projection of their film *Workers Leaving the Lumière Factory in Lyon*. Nearly one hundred and thirty years later, Paris can boast over four hundred cinema screens, so there is no shortage of choice!

Here Mathilde introduces the people who are important in her cultural life in Paris.

Guillaume Gallienne

He can play Pierre Bergé in *Yves Saint Laurent*, Argan on stage at the Comédie Française, or his mother in his film *Les Garçons et Guillaume, à table!*, which sold three million tickets. For a decade, his voice has introduced the classics to a large radio audience on France Inter. Guillaume Gallienne is not only a great actor, but also a playwright, screenwriter, and director. Since 2005, he has been a member of the Comédie Française. While the company's mission is to perform all kinds of theater from every period, both French and foreign, in the public imagination it is associated with the seventeenth-century classics, and especially with Molière, whose plays it has performed for over three hundred years.

Mathilde: "He's one of our finest actors. To see him perform in anything is a privilege. He takes you to another world. Guillaume is more than a friend; I think of him as one of the family. Genuine, warm, and witty, he has a brilliant mind."

230.

The Opéra Comique Gala

It was on the stage of the Opéra Comique, on March 3, 1875, that Georges Bizet's *Carmen* was first performed, scandalizing the Parisian bourgeoisie before going on to become the world's most performed opera. This was also where Offenbach's *Tales of Hoffmann* had its premiere.

Parisians are generous and enthusiastic in their support of their temples of culture, and the social calendar is studded with gala evenings for which patrons mobilize their efforts to support institutions, museums, theaters, and libraries. Thanks to its president, Christine d'Ornano, Mathilde sits on the organizing committee for the annual Opéra Comique Gala. Every year, they gather with benefactors in the Salle Favart to see an iconic performance from the Opéra Comique repertoire, followed by a dinner in the theater foyer created by chef Alain Passard, holder of three Michelin stars. This sumptuous and little-known theater is well worth a visit.

RIGHT
Mathilde photographed at the Opéra Comique Gala dinner.
FAR RIGHT
The magnificent ceiling painting by Raphaël Collin and Édouard Toudouze in the foyer of the Opéra Comique, home to both sung and spoken-word performances.

Éric and Nicolas Altmayer

After sharing a bedroom for much of their childhood—they are the youngest of six siblings—Éric and Nicolas now share an office. In 1996, the two brothers founded their audiovisual production company, Mandarin. The company is famed for the diversity of its productions, including *Brice de Nice*, *OSS 117*, *Saint Laurent* by Bertrand Bonello, the films of François Ozon, and, more recently, television series including *Validé* and *Cœur noir*.

Nicknamed "the twin towers"—both are over six feet (1.9m) tall—they are great champions of French cinema. And if Nicolas shares his office with his brother, he also shares his life with Mathilde.

"If Paris was a film: *Amélie* by Jean-Pierre Jeunet; *Paris* by Cédric Klapisch; *Avenue Montaigne* by Danièle Thompson, for its views of elegant Paris; *Four Bags Full* by Claude Autant-Lara; *An American in Paris* by Vincente Minnelli, for its views of eternal Paris."

PAGE 236
Audrey Hepburn and
Fred Astaire in *Funny Face*.
PAGE 237
The Moulin Rouge,
the most famous
of Paris cabarets.
ABOVE
The poster for the François
Ozon film *Mon Crime*
(*The Crime is Mine*),
produced by Éric
and Nicolas Altmayer,
displayed on one of
the city's iconic Morris
advertising columns.

RIGHT AND FACING PAGE
The brothers chose to be
photographed outside the
legendary Louxor cinema,
built by Henri Zipcy and
opened in 1921. Restored
by Philippe Pumain,
it reopened in 2013 and
shows mostly arthouse
movies.

239.

"Three cult films about Paris: *The 400 Blows* and *The Last Metro* by François Truffaut; *Breathless* by Jean-Luc Godard." – **Vanessa van Zuylen**

Vanessa van Zuylen

A childhood friend of Mathilde and a serial entrepreneur, Vanessa founded the wonderful magazine *L'Insensé* in 1991. It offered high-quality content until 2016, with each issue exploring a theme—friendship, dreams, the body, happiness—with a cover illustration by Pierre Alechinsky. In 2000, the magazine became *L'Insensé-Photo*, focusing on contemporary photography. In parallel, Vanessa founded *Version Femina*, a supplement to *Le Journal du Dimanche*, and asked Mathilde to be fashion editor. Then came a publishing house in Japan and the launch of *Personality* magazine.

In 2013, Vanessa, a cinema-lover since her teenage years, also became a film producer. Her first film, *Up For Love*, starring Jean Dujardin and Virginie Efira and released in 2016, was a success. Her next project was the ambitious biopic *Eiffel*, with Romain Duris in the title role, and now she completes filming a series based on the life of Marie-Antoine Carême, chef to the statesman and diplomat Charles-Maurice de Talleyrand-Périgord and father of French haute cuisine.

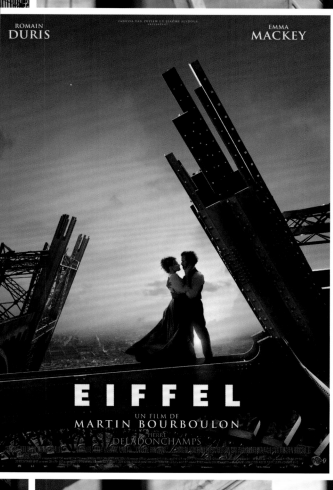

ROMAIN
DURIS

EMMA
MACKEY

EIFFEL

UN FILM DE
MARTIN BOURBOULON

PIERRE
DELADONCHAMPS

Sidonie Dumas

The CEO of Gaumont maintains a discreet presence
on both mainstream and social media.

Sidonie decided to go into cinema during filming
of *The Big Blue*, starting out as an intern in Luc Besson's
production company before moving into acquisitions at
Warner Bros in Los Angeles. She was twenty-four when
she joined Gaumont in Paris, worked her way up through
the ranks and establishing herself as the natural heir
to the film production and distribution company that is
as old as cinema itself. Appointed CEO in 2004, she has
brought Gaumont into the twenty-first century by
diversifying and restructuring, while keeping production
as its core business. And like all producers, her aim is
to make viewers want to see movies in theaters.

"She's reserved, daring, and a risk-taker, which has
earned her the respect and admiration of her peers
in France and abroad," Mathilde concludes. "She's also
charming, ultra-feminine, has exquisite taste, and is
a sublime cook. I share my secrets with her, and I have
complete trust in her."

Élisabeth Quin

A journalist and writer, she occupies an enviable position
in the French audiovisual landscape. She has been
a film critic, has hosted radio and television programs
on cinema, and has taken part in some of France's most
celebrated programs, including *Le Masque et la Plume*
on France Inter and *Rive droite / Rive gauche* on Paris
Première, before adding fashion to her repertoire.

Élisabeth has written several autobiographical books,
in which she uses self-effacing humor to downplay a
sometimes harsh and painful reality. We photographed
her on the set of *28 minutes*, the excellent current affairs
program she has presented on Arte since 2012.

Mathilde: "Her voice is captivating, enveloping.
I'm intimidated by her culture and her infallible memory.
She has announced that she has a disease that may
gradually rob her of her sight, and yet there's nothing
she doesn't see. She's one of those people you can't
get enough of."

Belle de Paris

"I see my body as my home: I live in it, I take care of it, I repair it." – Mathilde

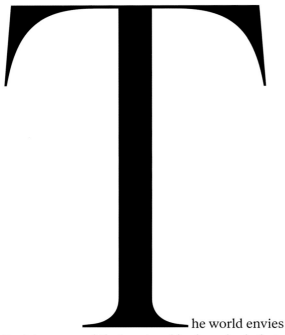

The world envies Parisiennes and their natural look—a look that often involves a great deal of effort, though it always appears effortless. Parisiennes somehow manage to pull off the tour de force of being elegant without being contrived. For centuries, Parisiennes have led the way in ideas of beauty, from Diane de Poitiers to Marie Antoinette and Gabrielle Chanel, and from Inès de la Fressange to Jeanne Damas, and all the women who feature in these pages. All have their beauty tips and secrets.

Mathilde is always on the lookout for new products, new protocols, new therapies, new venues. Well-versed in alternative therapies, she is ready to try them without preconceptions. And she is generous with her contacts and has always shared them, even before the dawn of Instagram.

Far more than beauty, it is the idea of wellness, or rather, of *being well*, that she pursues. Of course, she can put her sunny energy and infectious cheerfulness down to her good nature, but she also owes them to a discipline that she's happy to embrace. Taking care of yourself means loving and respecting yourself. It's not a discipline that is prescriptive, rather it grounds her, soothes her, makes her happy. It's what helps her to do her job according to one infallible formula: looking after everything around her and enjoying a good laugh every day.

PAGES 248–249
Mathilde at the Dior spa in the Hôtel Cheval-Blanc Paris, relaxing in the most beautiful swimming pool in Paris, reserved exclusively for clients of the hotel. The mosaics of the one-hundred-foot (thirty-meter) pool were executed by hand by Michael Mayer.

ABOVE
Mathilde's beauty shelves.
FACING PAGE
Bathtime.
"My bathroom has become my sacred space, where I recharge my batteries."

Charvet Paris

An institution, synonymous with Parisian chic, Charvet has been
dressing the elegant man- about-town since 1838. The client list
of the tailor who made shirts for Marcel Proust is an international
Who's Who, including John F. Kennedy, Bernard-Henri Lévy,
and Charles de Gaulle. The bespoke tailoring experience has
remained unchanged for decades in their Place Vendôme premises,
where they also offer impeccably cut off-the-peg suits in the finest
fabrics, selected from a choice of no fewer than six thousand.
Women commandeered their designs long ago, way ahead
of the vogue for boyfriend shirts.

"What I love about Charvet is their men's shirts. I steal them
from my husband and give them a feminine twist. Nothing could
look more chic on a woman than a man's striped robe or nightshirt."

Buly

In 2014, Victoire de Taillac and her husband, Ramdane Touhami, gave a new lease of life to the dispensary founded in 1803 by the perfumer Jean-Vincent Bully—inspiration for the eponymous protagonist in Balzac's *César Birotteau*—who launched a vogue for an aromatic vinegar invented by his father.

Victoire remembers that when they opened their first boutique, on Rue Bonaparte, Mathilde was one of their first customers. With her enquiring mind, she was won over from day one by their beautifully packaged products promising universal and enduring beauty secrets.

Buly assistants, with their training in the arts of calligraphy, engraving, and embossing, ensure that here beauty is a truly personal affair. A visit to Buly is an experience that is timeless, amid a décor skillfully dreamed up by Ramdane's marketing genius.

LEFT
Victoire de Taillac, joint founder of Buly, in the first Buly boutique on Rue Bonaparte.
ABOVE AND FACING PAGE
Details of the boutique.

254.

"When we opened our first boutique on Rue Bonaparte, Mathilde was one of our first customers." – **Victoire de Taillac**

Muse & Heroine

Muse & Heroine was the brainchild of founder Janine Knizia, at that time already head of Europe's first clean beauty showroom for professionals, based in Paris and specializing in the launch of green, luxury, and niche beauty brands. During the Covid-19 pandemic, she decided to offer a means of direct access for consumers. So in autumn 2022, she opened this sanctuary in the heart of the Marais, where she offers "clean-ical" brands, products with active ingredients that are scientifically endorsed and that she has personally tested. Much more than merely a boutique, this avant-garde space, with beauty, wellbeing, longevity, science, and spirituality at its heart, is a meeting place for a holistic community.

ESSUYEZ VOS PIE

ABOVE, RIGHT, AND FACING PAGE
Janine Knizia chose premises in the heart of the Marais for her concept store dedicated to clean beauty. Mathilde comes for regular facial treatments in her showroom, which resembles a chic and stylish Parisian apartment.

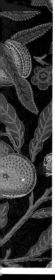

Diptyque

A bazaar of pretty things. The three founders, Desmond Knox-Leet, Christiane Montadre-Gautrot, and Yves Coueslant, all artists in their fields, took the name for their brand from the architecture of their historic premises at 34 Boulevard Saint-Germain: in its two symmetrical windows (not uncommon for a store) they saw a perfect diptych—*diptyque* in French. While the house logo's dancing letters and oval vignette inspired by a Roman shield, designed by Desmond, were immediately recognizable, it was, above all, the freedom and poetry of their creations that assured Diptyque's worldwide success. The art of perfume and *art de vivre* were united as one.

Everyone has their favorite fragrances, and Mathilde is no exception: Baies, Tubéreuse, or Lys, depending on the season. At home she has a cupboard filled with her favorite candles, and her spacious living room is always perfumed by her fragrance of the moment.

FACING PAGE
The décor of the first Diptyque boutique, opened in 1961 at 34 Boulevard Saint-Germain. In 1963, Diptyque offered its first candles for sale, followed in 1968 by its first perfume, L'Eau.
LEFT
Henri Fournier, was shop manager and legendary presence behind the counter for Diptyque for decades.
PAGES 262–263
In the world of Diptyque, the colorful packaging is as elegant as the contents it protects.

Paris, *mon Amour*

"For those like us who share such a great love, Paris is very small." – Jacques Prévert, *Children of Paradise*, 1945.

P

aris is *the* city of romance, the city of romantics par excellence. How many marriage proposals, engagements, celebrations, couples, and honeymoons has Paris witnessed?

French Romanticism found its embodiment in poetry, plays, and paintings. French is the language of love, and every nook and corner of Paris is a backdrop for declaring or falling in love.

It could be in front of Rodin's *The Kiss*, installed in the mansion where Rodin lived, in the shadow of Les Invalides. Converted into the Musée Rodin immediately after his death in 1919, following his wishes, this magical place houses his collections, which he gifted to the French state, and tourists and local residents flock there.

Another spot favored by lovers is the Medici Fountain, commissioned by Marie de Medici in 1630 from her fellow Italian Thomas Francini to adorn the gardens of her sumptuous new residence, the Palais du Luxembourg. It now lies in the shadow of the palace, seat of the French parliament, and since 1862 its central niche has held Auguste Ottin's sculpture, *Polyphemus Surprising Acis and Galatea*.

In Paris, lovers kiss in the street, in front of the most beautiful monuments, on the bridges over the Seine, on public benches. After all, isn't the English for *un baiser amoureux* a "French kiss"?

PAGE 264
The Medici Fountain, the iconic monument in the Jardin du Luxembourg.

PAGE 265
Mathilde and her partner, Nicolas, strolling hand in hand through the streets of Paris.

FACING PAGE
With her lightness, humor, allure, nonchalance, and love of dressing up, Mathilde could have been the inspiration for one of Kiraz's heroines.

PAGES 268–269
L'Amour Gagne Toujours (*Love Always Wins*), street art by Toqué Frères.

266.

Alexandra Van Houtte

Half-French and half-British, Alexandra grew up in Paris, where she still lives. In 2016, this cheerful and dynamic stylist-turned-entrepreneur launched Tagwalk, a searchable database of fashion image collections that also identifies trends and advises on labels, and that has become highly valued for its relevance.

On April 1, 2023, Alexandra married David Franck in the town hall of the 6th arrondissement, which stands on one of the most beautiful squares in Paris, opposite the church of Saint-Sulpice. Built in several stages between 1660 and 1870, the church is unusual for the mismatched towers of its west face, built to the designs of two different architects.

Mathilde: "Alexandra is direct, she tells it like it is. She keeps me in touch with youth culture and introduces me to lots of young Parisian artists, like the illustrator Marie-Victoire de Bascher. She's one of a new generation of women who are very inspiring."

"It's a city that makes you want to fall in love."

– Mathilde

FACING PAGE
Laurence Borel,
illustration by
Marc-Antoine Coulon.

RIGHT
Mathilde on the way
to dinner at Maxim's,
casual and relaxed
in an evening dress on
Place de la Concorde.

Acknowledgments

This book, which I conceived as a way of sharing my ideal Paris and a certain art of life, has afforded me the immense privilege of meeting and catching up with some exceptional people, without whom this adventure would not have been the same. I would like to extend my sincere gratitude to all of them for accompanying me on a unique journey that has proved so rewarding.

Special thanks are therefore due to all the individuals who feature in this book. With their unique qualities, their generosity and availability, their skills and their conversation, they have all played their part in the enthusiasm and passion that for so many years have driven my life in Paris. I am so proud to share these pages with them.

I am grateful to my mother Françoise Favier and my uncle Gilles Dufour, for passing on their insatiable desire to infuse life with beauty. To my sisters Victoire de Castellane-Lenthal and Pauline Favier-Henin, and my children Héloïse and Carlo Agostinelli, for their love and unfailing support. To Nicolas Altmayer for sharing my life.

I would like to extend my warmest thanks to the teams at Christian Dior with whom I have been fortunate enough to work for so many years: to Delphine Arnault, Maria Grazia Chiuri, and Olivier Bialobos, and to my invaluable team, starting with my "mellow" Hélène Poirier, followed by Aline Dos Santos, Marine Szwaja, Christèle Pigeon, Tamia Gopee, Lucie Le Texier, Aurore Da Silva, Emma Le Forestier, and Claire Lucas.

I am also grateful to my friends, for their trust and their kindness. They have always been there, and they will recognize themselves in these pages.

Thank you to Bertrand Burgalat, Vanessa Seward-Burgalat and Natalie David-Weill for their absolute confidence.

My sincere thanks go to Jolanta Cedro for making me look beautiful, to Anne-Louise Pothier, International Director of Dior Spa and Wellness, to Janine Knizia, founder of Muse & Heroine, to Cynthia Franck, and to models Apolline Rocco-Fohrer and Maya Teodora Savic.

Many thanks also to the Association Cultuelle Orthodoxe Russe, Alexander Nevsky Cathedral, Palais Galliera, École 42, Galerie Pixi, Au Bain Marie, Hôtel Amour, Le Grand Véfour, Aux Crus de Bourgogne, Moulin Rouge, Le Louxor Cinema, Hôtel Cheval Blanc Paris, Musée Rodin, and Musée Picasso.

Finally, I would like to thank Frédérique Dedet for always finding the right words; photographer Pascal Chevallier, whose vision and patience were indispensable; and at Éditions Flammarion, Style & Design Collection, Suzanne Tise-Isoré, Bernard Lagacé, Aude Schlosser, and Cécile Baribaud, without whom this book would never have come to fruition.

A percentage of the book's sales will be donated to the Rafaël Institute, Europe's leading center for integrative medicine, which provides free support for patients and their carers, during and after cancer.

Photographic credits

t: top, b: bottom, l: left, r: right, c: center
All photographs in this book were taken by Pascal Chevallier except those on the following pages:
Endpaper: © Grey Zisser; p. 11: © Mathilde Favier archives; p. 13: © Mathilde Favier archives; p. 14: © Mario Testino, © Jean Marc Manson; p. 14b: © Mathilde Favier archives; p. 15c: © Grey Zisser; p. 15b: © Manuela Pavesi; pp. 16–17: © Andrew Durham; pp. 18–19: © Mathilde Favier archives; p. 20: © May Meng; p. 26c: © Pierre et Gilles: *Gilles Dufour*, 1979 (Les Fonds À Fleurs collection); p. 30tl: © Mathilde Favier archives; p. 33tr: © Pascal Hinous; p. 33bl: © Pascal Hinous; p. 33br: © Mathilde Favier archives; p. 34t: © Christian Dior; p. 35tl: © François Halard; p. 36b: © Bloom Paris; p. 40: © Association Willy Maywald/Adagp, Paris, 2023; pp. 54–55: © Tom Watson; pp. 62–63: © Mathilde Favier archives; p. 64l: © Mathilde Favier archives; p. 74c: © François Halard; p. 79b: © Julio Piatti; pp. 102–103c: © Casa Lopez for Maison Thevenon; p. 118: © All rights reserved; p. 119: © Mathilde Favier archives; pp. 128–129c: © Tatiana de Nicolay; p. 134tr: © Photo12/Alamy/ Hirarchivum Press; pp. 136–137: © Kasia Matenska, 2023; p. 142g: © Charlotte Robin; p. 154tl: © Harry Gruyaert; p. 155br: © Vincent Ferrané; p. 165tl: © Benedetta Chiala; p. 165tr: © Charles Negre/Lambert Lambert – Set Design © Juliette Zakowetz/Lambert Lambert; p. 165bc: © Sophie Rolland; p. 183c: © BnF; p. 190: © Castor Florist; p. 191: © Raphaël Dautigny; p. 206bl: © Bernard Lagacé; p. 214l: © Cecil Mathieu; pp. 226–227l: © Sacha Floch Poliakoff, 2022; p. 229: © Mariela Medina; p. 236: © Photo12/Alamy/PictureLux/The Hollywood Archive/Paramount; p. 238c: © Anthony Rauchen; p. 241c: © VVZ Production, © Pathé; p. 244c: © Photo12/Alamy/Shawshots/Franco-London Films; p. 267: © Denoël Editions, 2001; p. 272l: © Jean Picon; p. 273: © Jean Picon; p. 281: © Mathilde Favier archives.

Artistic credits

Pp. 2–3: © Vanessa Seward; p 15tr: © Marc-Antoine Coulon; p. 25: © Claude Lalanne/Adagp, Paris, 2023 (*La Pomme*); p. 26c: © Pierre et Gilles (portrait); p. 29: © Claude Lalanne/Adagp, Paris, 2023 (*La Pomme*), © Karl Lagerfeld (portrait); p. 34bl: © Victoire de Castellane (self-portrait); p. 36: © Bruno Capacci (table); p. 58: © Victoire de Castellane (self-portrait); p. 66: © Mario Testino (picture); p. 71br: © Lynda Draper; p. 72: © Maurizio Cattelan (painting); p. 72-73c: © Keith Haring (painting); p. 73tr: © Yves Saint Laurent (drawing), © Matt Wilt (sculpture); p. 76bl: © Samuel Mazy (bronze and porcelain tree), © Patrice Dangel (low table), © Hélène Dalloz-Bourguignon (drawing); pp. 78–79: © Patrice Dangel (Volutes coffee table), © Samuel Mazy (branch and ceiling light), © Claude Lalanne (pair of chairs); p. 79b: © Armelle Fabre (plaster bust); p. 80: © Claude Lalanne/Adagp, Paris, 2023 (*Choupatte*); pp. 80–81: © Mattia Bonetti (carpet); p. 83 : © Paul Iribe (armchair); Alberto Giacometti/Adagp, Paris, 2023 (sculpture), © Sam Szafran/Adagp, Paris, 2023 (painting); p. 92: © Chale Ado/Adagp, Paris, 2023 (coffee table), © Agostino Bonalumi/Adagp, Paris, 2023 (painting); p. 96: © Paolo Venini (ceiling lights); p. 103: © Kim Moltzer (chair); p. 105: © Hervé Van der Straeten (ceiling light); p. 109: © Audrey Guimard and Camille Coléon (fountain); p. 143: © Latifa Echakhch (bench); p. 146cr: © Chloé Bolloré; p. 147: © Chloé Bolloré; p.152t: © Jean-François Fourtou/Adagp, Paris, 2023 (*Papillon*); pp. 152–153: © Ricardo Macarron/ Adagp, Paris, 2023 (paintings); p. 206: © Succession Picasso 2023; p. 207: © Alberto Giacometti/Adagp, Paris, 2023; pp. 212–213: © Alice Gavalet (sculptures); p. 213: © Pietro Ruffo (on the wall); pp. 268–269: © Toqué Frères; p. 277: © Marc-Antoine Coulon.

Every effort has been made to identify photographers and copyright holders of the images reproduced in this book.
Any errors or omissions referred to the publisher will be corrected in subsequent printings.

EXECUTIVE DIRECTOR
Suzanne Tise-Isoré
Style & Design Collection

EDITORIAL COORDINATION
Aude Schlosser

EDITORIAL ASSISTANT
Cécile Baribaud

GRAPHIC DESIGN
Bernard Lagacé

TRANSLATED FROM THE FRENCH BY
Barbara Mellor

COPY EDITING AND PROOFREADING
Lindsay Porter

PRODUCTION
Élodie Conjat

COLOR SEPARATION
Les Artisans du Regard, Paris

PRINTING
C&C Offset, China

Simultaneously published in French as *Mathilde à Paris*.

© Éditions Flammarion, Paris, 2024

English-language edition
© Éditions Flammarion, Paris, 2024

Éditions Flammarion
82, rue Saint-Lazare
75009 Paris
editions.flammarion.com
@styleanddesignflammarion
@flammarioninternational

L.01EBTN001052
24 25 26 4 3 2
ISBN: 978-2-08-043332-9
Legal deposit: 04/2024

Très chère Mathilde,

Pour envoyer des pensées,
de l'amour et des fleurs !

Hadrien

DIOR

uelle année incroyable... Merci à vous tous, du fond du cœur !

votre talent, votre inépuisable passion et votre engagement constant,
mmes devenus la marque la plus désirable de l'univers du luxe, et avons
us nos précédents records. Nous pouvons tous en être très fiers.

lant, notre voyage ne fait que commencer, et bien d'autres défis, aussi
es qu'excitants, nous attendent. J'ai hâte de les relever avec cette incroyable
que je suis si fier de diriger.

ons à rêver chez Dior.

souhaite, ainsi qu'à vos familles, de magnifiques fêtes de fin d'année.

Pietro Beccari

Fiori

Ma panthère

te voila parée comme un...

Voici de jolis soolices...
qui, je l'espère, tient à la...
Avec toute mon amitié Xx
Grégoire

29 II

Mathilde,

I really enjoyed meeting you
you have the best vibe!
Be well + healthy and continued
success!

Until next time,
Jens

VICTORIA BO...

MERRY C...
AND HAPPY

Amai...

MARIA G

OLIVIER BIALOBOS
CHIEF COMMUNICATION OFFICER

Ma Fanette,
un peu de douceur
en cette période si
étrange

Christian Dior
COUTURE

Marie -

Pour m...

HAPPY NEW YEAR !
WITH LOVE

Mariaghazie

Chèr...

ISABELLA C...

Une peu...
pent et
Xavier,
Loquet

XNatale 2019

Elisabetta Beccari

Mathilde,

Love to you
Family !
Natale.

Elisabetta

! ☺

Chère Mathilde,

Merci d'avoir...

Je T'aime

Merci Matilde
Je T'aime
- Savannah
♡

50, RUE DE LA BIENFAISANCE , VIII

Mathilde chérie

7 nov 2019

Perdu son père en...

Bon anniver
math
Je t'embrasse
affectueus
ton frère

Merci encore my L...

Merci pour ton 💋
quotidien qui me met du
Baume au ♥...

Leila

pour te protéger du froid
car tu es un...

Joyeux Noël.

Leila Tumaa

GHERARDO FELLONI

Chère Mathilde,

C'ÉTAIT UN VRAI PLAISIR DE
DÎNER AVEC TOI !!
LA NOUVELLE LOVE VIVIER Pour TOI...
" J'AI PAS RESISTÉ !! QUE CE CŒUR
TE VA À MERVEILLE !! " G. ♥

7. VII 22

MUSE & ...

KIM JONES

Dear Mathilde

DEAR MATHILDE
HAPPY BIRTHDAY !
WITH LOVE

L'INSENSÉ FILMS